A LOAD OF BALLS

A LOAD OF
BALLS
FOOTBALL'S FUNNY SIDE

JOHN SCALLY

MAINSTREAM
PUBLISHING

EDINBURGH AND LONDON

First published in Great Britain in 2009 by
MAINSTREAM PUBLISHING COMPANY
(EDINBURGH) LTD
7 Albany Street
Edinburgh EH1 3UG

ISBN 9781845964375

This edition published 2010 for Index Books Ltd

A catalogue record for this book is
available from the British Library

Typeset in Big Noodle and Sabon

Printed in Great Britain by
CPI Mackays, Chatham, ME5 8TD

*To the inspirational John Hancox, who despite
the minor inconveniences of having had his right
leg amputated as a result of his diabetes and being
partially sighted and having had a kidney transplant
two years ago still travels from Ireland to beautiful
downtown Bramall Lane every two weeks to see his
beloved Sheffield United play, and to his daughter
Barbara, who runs the Sheffield United Irish
Supporters Club, the Irish Blades.*

CONTENTS

GLOSSARY

FOOTBALL MADE SIMPLE

Football is a technical game with its own specialised vocabulary. Many people do not fully appreciate the nuances of football-speak. The following glossary of terms may help readers to understand this book more easily.

WHEN A PUNDIT SAYS:
This wonderfully historic ground . . .
What the pundit really means is:
It's a proper dump.

WHEN A PUNDIT SAYS:
You have to admire his loyalty to the club.
What the pundit really means is:
No other club would take him.

WHEN A PUNDIT SAYS:
Few players show such flair.
What the pundit really means is:
He is a complete show-off.

WHEN A PUNDIT SAYS:
He's a player who relies on instinct.
What the pundit really means is:
He hasn't a brain in his head.

WHEN A PUNDIT SAYS:
This match was not without its moments.
What the pundit really means is:
It would be more exciting to watch with the TV turned off.

WHEN A PUNDIT SAYS:
He has an interesting temperament.
What the pundit really means is:
He's a complete nutcase.

WHEN A PUNDIT SAYS:
He shows great economy around the ball.
What the pundit really means is:
He never gets near the thing.

WHEN A PUNDIT SAYS:
The long-standing servant . . .
What the pundit really means is:
He must soon be entitled to free bus travel.

WHEN A PUNDIT SAYS:
He's as complex as a jigsaw puzzle.
What the pundit really means is:
He falls to pieces in the box.

WHEN A PUNDIT SAYS:
You have to admire his competitive spirit.
What the pundit really means is:
He is a psychopath.

WHEN A PUNDIT SAYS:
He's a seasoned veteran.
What the pundit really means is:
He's past it.

WHEN A PUNDIT SAYS:
He showed great promise as a teenager.
What the pundit really means is:
He's totally useless now.

WHEN A PUNDIT SAYS:
The referee had a poor view of the incident.
What the pundit really means is:
The ref is as blind as a bat.

WHEN A PUNDIT SAYS:
He has a distinctive look.
What the pundit really means is:
He has a face only his mother could love.

INTRODUCTION

'Football is all very well as a game for rough girls, but it is hardly suitable for delicate boys.'

Oscar Wilde

Football punditry is the art of looking for trouble, finding it everywhere, diagnosing it wrongly and applying unsuitable remedies. Football fans have long been exercised by the verbal shortcomings of pundits, as is evident in a letter to *The Guardian* on Mike Channon's and Emlyn Hughes' performances during the 1986 World Cup: 'Conjugate the verb "done great": I done great. He done great. We done great. They done great. The boy Lineker done great.'

One lesson football pundits have sadly never learned is that a good time to keep your mouth shut is when you are in deep water. As a result, they have talked themselves into trouble more often than most people have hot dinners.

Brendan Behan claimed: 'Critics are like eunuchs in a harem: they know how it's done, they've seen it done every day, but they're unable to do it themselves.' That may be true in the theatre, but not so much in the world of punditry. The definition that I feel best sums up some football pundits is the late Peter Ustinov's: 'A critic is someone who searches for ages for the wrong word, which, to his eternal credit, he invariably finds.' If there is a wrong word to be found, you can bet your bottom dollar the football pundit will find it and pay the penalty for his remarks! After he has made a faux pas yet

again, the only thing he has to console him is that he doesn't
have a monopoly on putting his foot in his mouth.

I have experienced the media's misdemeanours at first
hand. One of my first books was reviewed in the *Irish Times*.
It should have been one of the great moments of my life, but
I was bemused to discover that I had had a name change
and that I was now 'Jean Scally'. I wrote a little note to the
then books editor and subsequent Booker Prize-winner, John
Banville, and informed him, 'Reports of my sex change have
been greatly exaggerated.'

The walls of waffle spawned by football have generated
enough natural gas to power the national grid. The beautiful
game never ceases to entertain, but sometimes the off-field
verbal antics surpass what happens on the pitch. We ought not
to, to quote George W. Bush, 'misunderestimate' the ability
of football personalities to get in a verbal muddle. We've
heard gems from managers like Kevin Keegan: 'People will
say that was typical [Manchester] City, which really annoys
me. But that's typical City, I suppose.' Then there are players
like former Aston Villa striker Dalian Atkinson: 'If I was still
at Ipswich, I wouldn't be where I am today.' And, of course,
there are the pundits, like Sky's Andy Gray: 'There was no
contact there, just a clash of bodies.'

There are the mathematically challenged, such as Chris
Coleman: 'Our destiny is in our own hands. We've got
six games left – two at home and three away.' There's the
puzzling, like Graeme Souness's observation: 'Matt Le Tissier
was a super striker of the ball, but he never played for a big
club. If he had, we'd be talking about him as a super striker of
the ball.' Then there's the *really* puzzling, like Rio Ferdinand's
comment: 'Gary Neville is the club captain but has been
injured for the best part of a year now, so Giggsy's taken on
the mantelpiece.'

As this book was being finished, news broke that
Manchester United had sold Ronaldo, described by the
Daily Mail as the 'Lily Savage' of football for his devotion to
fashion, to Real Madrid for £80 million. It reminded me of
Chris Waddle's comment: 'The one thing Cristiano Ronaldo

has is pace, quick feet and a great eye for goal.' Given the scale of the transfer fee, I wondered if for that money he could turn water into wine. On further consideration, given his history of petulance, it is more likely he can turn water into whine.

Many of the anecdotes in this collection are strange but true. However, the veracity of some of the stories would not measure up to that expected in a court of law. These stories are based on real events; only the facts have been changed! Many of these tales of the unexpected are shamelessly apocryphal and some are simply jokes. They are not meant to be statements of fact but intended to give a laugh or at least bring a smile. There are times when I have gone for the Dorothy Parker approach: 'I don't care what is written about me so long as it isn't true.'

It is said that humour and good taste are often mutually exclusive. That is probably particularly the case with football humour. For those who love political correctness, this is not the book. Hopefully, though, it is the book for those who love the beautiful game. It was Oscar Wilde who pointed out that no comment is in bad taste if it is amusing.

Quentin Crisp wrote: 'There are three reasons for becoming a writer: the first is that you need the money; the second that you have something to say that you think the whole world should know; the third is that you can't think what to do with the long winter evenings.' I would like to think that a fourth reason is to provide readers with something to do during the long winter evenings. In its own small way, this book attempts to do just that, while celebrating the fun that is attached to football and giving people a laugh or two. So smile and the football world will smile with you.

1

POSH AND BECKS

⚽

'Alex Ferguson is the best manager I've ever had at this level. Well, he's the only manager I've actually had at this level. But he's the best manager I've ever had.'

David Beckham

To many, David Beckham represents the best of British, as is evident in Hugh Grant's description of England in the smash film *Love Actually* as: 'The country of Shakespeare, Churchill, the Beatles, Sean Connery, Harry Potter. David Beckham's right foot. David Beckham's left foot, come to that.'

Becks is among the new English royalty, a superstar and a brand as well as a footballer. It is difficult to think of a sportsman more interested in fashion, hence the joke about the World Cup in 1998 – that the real reason Posh Spice was allowed to visit him in France for 'morale purposes' was not because he was upset about being dropped for England's opening match but because he'd missed the Armani summer sale in Bond Street! In hard times, Beckham favours retail therapy and goes to the shopping mall. When the going gets tough, the tough go shopping.

As a boy, though, Becks' fashion sense wasn't so well developed. One story goes back to his early school days. As the rest of his class are leaving at the end of a winter day, Becks remains behind sobbing.

'What's the matter, David?' his teacher asks.

'I can't find my boots!' Becks cries.

The teacher looks in the cloakroom and finds a pair of boots. 'Are these yours?'

'No,' Becks replies.

The teacher and David search all over the room. Finally, the teacher asks, 'Are you sure these boots aren't yours?'

'They aren't mine,' the distraught Beckham replies. 'Mine had snow on them.'

Becks' supposed intellectual limitations have been unintentionally confirmed by his own words – including:

'My parents have always been there for me, ever since I was about seven.'

GARY NEWBON: 'David, was Wayne Rooney disappointed to lose his youngest goal-scorer record on Monday to the young Swiss striker?'
BECKS: 'No, but I'm sure it'll make him even more determined to get it back against Portugal tonight.'

'It was really difficult for us playing in the midday sun with that three o'clock kick-off.'

'I definitely want Brooklyn to be christened, but I don't know into what religion yet.'

INTERVIEWER: 'Are you a volatile player?'
BECKS: 'Well, I can play in the centre, on the right and occasionally on the left side.'

On his first season in America: 'It's been great so far, very positive and smooth apart from . . . the season.'

'That was in the past. We're in the future now.'

TESTING TIMES

One day at school, the young Beckham is taking an important exam. His friend Gary is in the same class, and he's none too bright. The test is a fill-in-the-blanks job and the last question reads: 'Old MacDonald had a _____.' Gary is stumped. Making sure the teacher isn't looking, he taps Becks on the shoulder and whispers, 'David, what's the answer to the last question?'

Becks laughs, then looks around to make sure the teacher hasn't noticed. He turns to Gary and in a low voice says, 'You're so stupid. Everyone knows that Old MacDonald had a farm.'

'Oh, yeah,' says Gary, 'I remember now.' He picks up his pen and goes to fill in the answer. Then he stops. Tapping Becks on the shoulder, he whispers, 'David, how do you spell "farm"?'

'You really are stupid. That's so easy,' whispers Becks. '"Farm" is "E-I-E-I-O".'

QUIET, PLEASE

Manchester United are playing Chelsea at Old Trafford. Early on, George Weah is adjudged to have fouled Jaap Stam at a corner and begins furiously shouting and remonstrating with the ref. Upon seeing this, David Beckham races up to Weah, puts a finger to his lips and says, 'Shhhh!' Then he bursts out laughing and runs off, leaving Weah in a state of bewilderment.

Shortly afterwards, Dwight Yorke scores after lax defending by Chelsea. George is furious and shouts at them to get their act together. Once again, Becks goes up to Weah, says, 'Shhhh!', starts wetting himself laughing and runs off. Weah turns to his equally bemused teammates but they all shrug their shoulders in confusion.

Before the interval, Weah loses his cool with the linesman after a controversial offside is given against him, and Becks repeats his strange act.

At the half-time whistle, Keane goes over to Beckham and says, 'What's all this about Weah?'

Becks whispers something in Keane's ear, to which Keane rolls his eyes and replies, 'No you f***ing idiot, he's a Liberian.'

GOLDENBALLS

Becks is often voted among the sexiest men alive, which raises the question: are there any sexy corpses? In any case, he's always seemed very comfortable with his sexuality, telling *Marie Claire* magazine, 'I can't dance, but I'm an animal in bed.' Meanwhile, Victoria has remarked of him wearing a sarong, 'It's nothing out of the ordinary. David wears my knickers as well. He's getting in touch with his feminine side . . . I call him Goldenballs.'

Becks is certainly on the ball when it comes to his wife's career as a singer in her post-Spice Girls phase, commenting: 'I've heard some of Victoria's new album and it's frightening.' Anyone who has heard her solo album knows exactly what he meant.

MOTHER-IN-LAW KNOWS BEST

After the Rebecca Loos scandal broke, Becks didn't speak to his wife in six months – he didn't like to interrupt her.

Of course, no marriage is without its rocky patches. One young man on the verge of getting married discovered that his mother-in-law was worried that he would develop a roving eye. He tried to reassure her by telling her that the marriage was made in heaven, but she only answered, 'So is thunder and lightning.'

In fairness to Becks, he is not the only sports star to be associated with Ms Loos. Former Wimbledon champion Pat Cash had trouble recalling if he'd ever slept with her, telling one tabloid, 'I'm 50 per cent sure I did . . . I just can't remember.'

RIGHT ON

Given Victoria's revelation about David sporting her underwear, it's perhaps no surprise that there's been speculation that it's Posh who wears the trousers in the relationship. Becks has always been happy to acknowledge that Victoria is his Miss Right, but perhaps he didn't realise that her first name was Always.

It's far from an unusual phenomenon. Take the story about the young couple whose friends knew as early as their wedding day who was going to be in charge.

The priest asked the bride: 'Do you take this man to be your husband?' and she said, 'I do.'

Then the priest asked the groom, 'Do you take this woman to be your wife?' and the bride said, 'He does.'

FORGIVEN NOT FORGOTTEN?

One day, Becks does something really stupid. Posh chews him out for it and Becks spends a few nights on the couch. Becks apologises, and they make up. However, from time to time, Posh mentions what he'd done. 'Honey,' Becks finally says one day, 'why do you keep bringing that up? I thought your policy was forgive and forget?'

Posh replies, 'It is. I just don't want you to forget that I've forgiven and forgotten.'

LOOKS CAN BE DECEIVING

A doctor examines Victoria, takes David aside and says, 'I don't like the look of your wife at all.'

Becks replies, 'Well, fair enough, but she's a great cook and really good with our children.'

KIDNAPPED

In 2002, a plot hatched to kidnap Posh was foiled at the last minute. Cynics suggested that real music fans had instigated the plot to ensure we would never have to listen to her tunes again.

After news of the kidnap attempt broke, a police spokesman stated, 'The Beckhams will now be the subject of intelligence monitoring.' Some remarked that hell would freeze over before the Beckhams and intelligence would ever be spoken of again in the one sentence.

Indeed, in April 2003, when it was widely reported that Becks was about to sign for Real Madrid, some unkind people had it that the couple had begun to prepare for the move by learning Italian!

MY LEFT FOOT

In a match against a Spanish team before the 2002 World Cup, Beckham injured a small bone in his left foot. The injury was a national talking point, with one paper urging fans to pray that he would recover in time for the competition and 'metatarsal' becoming a household word. In the aftermath of the fuss, Queen Margaret University College in Edinburgh announced that it was to run a special course on the metatarsal. Hoping to entice young people into the field of podiatry, staff at their human-performance lab would soon be staging 'The Story of Beckham's Foot'.

UNTO US A CHILD IS BORN

In 2001, Posh and Becks agreed to be grilled by Sacha Baron-Cohen as Ali G for Comic Relief. Millions watched the interview, which the comedy character began by telling David, 'Now, just because it's Comic Relief, doesn't mean you can speak in a silly voice.'

He went on to enquire of Becks, 'It must be amazing going out with a Spice Girl, but in an ideal world – and no disrespect to your bitch – wouldn't you rather be with Baby?'

Asking Posh about the couple's son, who was then approaching his second birthday, Ali G wondered, 'Does Brooklyn like your music, or is he getting a bit old for it now?'

He followed that up with, 'Is your little boy starting to put whole sentences together?'

Victoria replied, 'He's learning the bits and pieces, so yeah.'

Ali G: 'And what about Brooklyn?'

BEST ON BECKS

Whatever has been said about his own linguistic deficiencies, David Beckham has inspired some wonderful comments. The following is an eclectic mix of Becks-inspired brilliance:

'I bet you two would love to play with him, what with those balls.'

Ray Wilkins sings the praises of David Beckham's crossing ability, leaving Joe Royle and Alan Shearer speechless

'Without being too harsh on David Beckham, he cost us the match.'

Ian Wright

'After tonight, England v. Argentina will be remembered for what a player did with his feet.'

Strangely prophetic Beckham-featuring Adidas advert broadcast in advance of the 1998 World Cup match in which Becks was sent off for kicking an Argentine player

'The midfield picks itself: Beckham, Scholes, Gerrard and A.N. Other.'

Phil Neal

'He's a girl's blouse.'

German journalist reacting to the news that David Beckham had been spotted leaving Beckingham Palace to attend a party wearing nail polish, not content with simply putting on a sarong or Posh's underwear

'Fingers crossed there's nothing broken.'

Alan Shearer on Beckham's hospital visit
for an X-ray on his injured hand

'Posh and Becks were so much in love after one year of going out that they were even thinking alike. For their first anniversary, they gave each other the exact same thing: earrings.'

Caller to Five Live phone-in

'It is important to remember that a player as talented as Beckham comes with a lot of baggage – most of it Louis Vuitton.'

Joseph O'Connor

'I have to watch my skin more and make sure that I look good and have had my hair done. I could easily lose my crown back to David Beckham if I'm not careful.'

Freddie Flintoff in 2005, on his status as a gay icon

'I would ask anyone to try to understand the world he lives in. We all have to accept that he is married to Spice Girl Victoria Adams – and I think he copes very well with it.'

Who knew Kevin Keegan had such sense and sensitivity?

'Becks hasn't changed since I've known him. He's always been a flash Cockney git.'

Ryan Giggs

SHAKESPEAREAN

After Becks' second son, Romeo, was born, speculation mounted as to what advice Dad would give his son when he played his first match. One Shakespeare scholar observed that if he handed him the number 4 jersey, he could adapt one of the most famous lines in English literature to 'Wear 4 out there, Romeo!'

LINGUISTIC PROBLEMS

After his move to Spain, Beckham tried to learn Spanish. One of the first phrases he picked up from his new Real Madrid teammates was '*hijo de puta*', which he took to be a fairly innocuous epithet. Unfortunately, the person Becks decided to try it out on was the linesman during a match against Murcia in 2004. Beckham was red-carded and seemed stunned at the hostility of the referee's reaction. The phrase means 'son of a whore'.

After the match, Murcia boss John Toshack said, 'He's obviously picked up a few words of Spanish after all! I bet he wishes he hadn't learned them as well as he had done now.'

Beckham later commented, 'I didn't realise what I had said was that bad. I had heard a few of my teammates say the same before me.'

A LITERARY DISASTER

There was a fire at the Beckhams' home. The good news, though, was that the library was the only room burned down. Both books were destroyed. David was devastated. Apparently, he had almost finished colouring one of them in.

THE WINE TASTES FINE

In 2008, David gave Victoria a vineyard for her birthday, and it was announced that she was to make her own wine.

To the description, 'rather less than full-bodied, somewhat expensive, nice nose but perhaps a little bitter', one wag remarked, 'Fair enough, but what's the wine like?'

LOST

Becks and his wife were driving in Canada and got lost. Finally, they arrived on the outskirts of a city. They saw an old man on the street, so Victoria let down her car window and asked, 'Excuse me, sir. Where are we?'

The man replied, 'Saskatoon, Saskatchewan.'

As Victoria rolled up the window, Becks turned to her and said, 'We really are lost. They don't even speak English here.'

THE JUROR

David Beckham is called up for jury service, and the selection process goes on and on, each side hotly contesting and dismissing potential jurors. David is called for questioning.

'Property holder?'

'Yes, I am, Your Honour.'

'Married or single?'

'Married for years, Your Honour.'

'Formed or expressed an opinion?'

'Not in many years, Your Honour.'

FANTASY FOOTBALLER

Posh and Becks are lying in bed in LA one night when he notices that she's bought a new book entitled *What 20 Million American Women Want*. He grabs it out of her hands and starts thumbing through the pages. Posh is a little annoyed, asking, 'Hey, what do you think you're doing?'

David calmly replies, 'I just wanted to see if they spelled my name right.'

A LETTER

Becks is renegotiating his contract in the States, and comes up with a clever way to try and get more money from the club. He writes a letter:

Dear Chairman,

Your club i$ really great. I am making lot$ of friend$ and $tudying tactic$ hard. With all my $tuff, I $imply can't think of anything I need, $o if you like, you can ju$t $end me a card, a$ I would love to hear from you.

Love, your $pecial player

The following response arrives a week later.

> Dear David,
> I kNOw that team tactics are eNOugh to keep even an hoNOrs student busy. Do NOt forget that the pursuit of kNOwledge is a NOble task and you can never study eNOugh.
>   Love, the chairman

THE PLAY'S THE THING

In 2009, Posh and Becks' celebrity lifestyle inspired a new play, *Macbecks*, which premiered in Dublin. Based *very* loosely on Shakespeare's *Macbeth*, the play begins with three man-hungry members of the Spice Witches who conjure up a hunk of soccer superstardom in the form of Macbecks, who soon falls under the spell of England football coach S'Alex. Macbecks' star is soaring until his girlfriend Poshoria and S'Alex fall out, and Poshoria persuades her man to slay his beloved 'dad' with comic results. At one point, S'Alex says to the Spice Witches, 'A plague on all your mock-Tudor mansions.'

HOT AND COLD

During his time at Man United, Beckham notices a Thermos flask during a shopping trip.

'What's that for?' he asks.

'It's to keep hot things hot and cold things cold,' replies the salesman.

Beckham buys one and takes it home to show Posh. With wonder in his voice, he tells her, 'It's to keep hot things hot and cold things cold.'

With a gasp of astonishment, she says, 'You ought to take it to work.'

So he takes it into training the following day.

'What you got there?' enquires Roy Keane.

'It's to keep hot things hot and cold things cold,' says Becks, with pride.

'That's a good idea,' says the captain. 'What have you got in it?'

'Coffee,' answers Becks. 'And some ice cream.'

2

ALEX VERSUS ARSÈNE

---

*'They say he's intelligent, right? Speaks five languages!
I've got a 15-year-old boy from the Ivory Coast
who speaks five languages!'*

Ferguson on Wenger

*'He doesn't interest me and doesn't matter to me at all. I
will never answer to any provocation from him any more.'*

Wenger on Ferguson

From throwing pizza to throwing tantrums, the often fractious relationship between Manchester United and Arsenal, and Alex Ferguson and Arsène Wenger, has brought much colour to the Premier League. Despite the seriousness of the managers' demeanour, individually and as a pair they have brought much mirth to football fans. If you are not convinced, consider the following evidence.

UNITED WE STAND

There's no doubt that Sir Alex Ferguson ('Sir Red Face' to Manchester City fans) is the manager of his generation. Fergie does not react well to defeat, which explains why it's always somebody else's fault when United lose. His most imaginative excuse was unquestionably when United lost 3–1 to Southampton in 1996. He blamed the kit. The new grey away strip, he claimed, meant that his players were unable to pick out their teammates.

Soccer's two other contenders for the award for best excuse are David James and Kenny Dalglish. James earned the nickname 'Calamity James' in his Liverpool days for a series of blunders that cost the Merseysiders dearly in 1997. His excuse was that he was fatigued because of the effects of ten-hour sessions on his PlayStation. A new riddle was born. What's the difference between Jesus and David James? Jesus saves.

The following year, non-league Stevenage held mighty Newcastle to a 1–1 draw. Their manager Kenny Dalglish's excuse was: 'Newcastle would have won but the balls were too bouncy.'

THE HORSE WHISPERER

Alex Ferguson is known for his love of racing, despite the protracted controversy over his ownership of the champion horse Rock Of Gibraltar.

One day, while on a walking holiday, Fergie stops alongside a field on a country road to rest for a few minutes. He is enjoying the peace when a horse comes over to the fence and begins to boast about his past.

'Yes, sir, I'm a fine horse. I've run in 25 races and won over £2 million. I keep my trophies in the barn.'

Fergie computes the value of having a talking horse, finds the animal's owner and offers to buy it.

'You don't really want that horse,' says the farmer.

'Yes, I do,' says Fergie, 'and I'll give you £100,000 for him.'

Recognising a good deal, the farmer says without hesitation, 'He's yours.'

While he writes out his cheque, Fergie asks, 'By the way, why wouldn't I want your horse?'

'Because,' says the farmer, 'he's a liar – he hasn't won a race in his life.'

CHASING CARS

One man who understands the pressure football managers are under is the 2007 and 2008 Open winner Padraig Harrington. No managers would share his mantra 'I want to focus on my focus' more than Alex Ferguson and Arsène Wenger. You can imagine that the two men are always looking for any stroke to put their opponent under pressure, hence the following story.

Alex and Arsène are sharing a car on the way to a promotional event a few days before their teams are to meet in the league. Ferguson's driving, but he hates wearing a seat belt and goes into a panic when he sees a policeman pulling them over. He says to Wenger, 'Quick, take the wheel. I've got to put my seat belt on.'

The policeman knocks on the window and says, 'Here, I noticed you weren't wearing your seat belt.'

Ferguson says, 'I was, but you don't have to take my word for it. This man here is a good honest man. Ask him – he'll tell you the truth. He doesn't lie about anything.'

The policeman says to Wenger, 'Well? How about it, sir?'

And Wenger says, 'I've known this man for twenty years and one thing I've learned in all that time is you never argue with him when he's drunk.'

DON'T LOOK BACK IN WENGER

Arsène Wenger rings Sir Alex after United's victory in the 2008 Champions League and asks, 'What's your top tip for winning the Champions League?'

Fergie says, 'You have to get your players doing the following drill: get loads of cones, placing them carefully around the field, loads of balls, have the players dribbling around the cones, doing one-twos, sidesteps, swerves, and kicking the ball into the net.'

After a few weeks, Sir Alex was surprised that Wenger hadn't rung him to thank him for his brilliant advice, so he rang Wenger and asked him how they'd got on.

'Not great. The cones beat us by six goals.'

ELEMENTARY

After years of wrangling between the two managers, it is suggested by a PR executive that Ferguson and Wenger should go on a camping trip in the interests of the images of their respective clubs. They set up their tent and fall asleep.

Some hours later, Ferguson wakes his new friend up.

'Arsène, look up at the sky and tell me what you see.'

Wenger replies, 'I see millions of stars.'

'What does that tell you?'

Wenger ponders for a minute. 'Astronomically speaking, it tells me that there are millions of galaxies and potentially billions of planets. Astrologically, it tells me that Saturn is in Leo. Time-wise, it appears to be approximately a quarter past three. Theologically, it's evident the Lord is all powerful and we are small and insignificant. Meteorologically, it seems that we will have a beautiful day tomorrow. What does it tell you?'

Ferguson is silent for a moment, then speaks: 'Arsène, you idiot, someone's stolen our tent.'

RADIO GA-GA

After the disappointing season of 2008–09, Arsène Wenger is so cheesed off that he decides to get away from it all and go for a holiday in the sun. At one stage, for a break from the beach, he goes into a hi-tech electrical store to buy a car radio, and the salesman says, 'This is the very latest model. It's voice activated. You just tell it what you want to listen to, and the station changes automatically. There's no need to take your hands off the wheel.'

When Wenger returns to England, he has it installed and the first morning back at work, as he's driving to the Emirates Stadium, he decides to test it. He says, 'Pop,' and the sound of the Beatles fills the car. He says, 'Country,' and instantly he's listening to Johnny Cash. Then, suddenly, a pedestrian steps off the pavement in front of him, causing him to swerve violently and shout, 'F***ing idiot!' Then the radio changes to a documentary on Alex Ferguson.

RACING CERTAINTY

As a keen racing fan, Sir Alex Ferguson once offered a trial to a horse who could talk, could out-dribble Ronaldo, could tackle tougher than Roy Keane and could do more tricks with the ball than Eric Cantona.

Fergie was about to offer the horse a contract but decided to set it one last test and instructed the equine star, 'Let's see you run without the ball.'

The horse shook its head sadly: 'If I could run, I'd be at the Epsom Derby, not in this dump.'

WORDS ARE ALL WE HAVE

Wenger and Ferguson have been the source and the subject of some good quotes. The following is my personal top ten.

1. 'Everyone knows that for us to get a penalty we need a certificate from the Pope and a personal letter from the Queen.'

    Alex Ferguson

2. 'He just floated over the ground like cocker spaniel chasing a piece of silver paper in the wind.'

    Fergie goes windy about Ryan Giggs

3. 'Everyone thinks they have the prettiest wife at home.'

    Arsène Wenger on Ferguson's claim that Manchester United play the most attractive football in England

4. 'His only weakness is that he thinks he doesn't have one.'

    Wenger on Ferguson

5. 'I have to sit down with him and see where we stand.'

    Wenger on a confusing meeting with Patrick Vieira

6. 'As long as no one scored, it was always going to be close.'

Arsène Wenger

7. 'At some clubs, success is accidental. At Arsenal, it is compulsory.'

Arsène Wenger

8. 'The new manager has given us unbelievable belief.'

Paul Merson extols the virtues of Wenger

9. 'When I say that he needs to stand up and be counted, I mean that he needs to sit down and have a look at himself in the mirror.'

Gary Mabbutt offers a pearl of wisdom to Sir Alex

10. 'He's so greedy for success that when his grandkids beat him at cards, he sends them to bed without any supper.'

Gary Pallister on Ferguson

ALL DONATIONS GRATEFULLY RECEIVED

A man on his way home from work was stuck in a traffic jam outside Old Trafford, and he thought to himself, 'Wow, the traffic seems worse than usual. Nothing's moving.'

He noticed a policeman walking back and forth between the lines of cars, so he rolled down his window and asked, 'Excuse me, what's the problem?'

The officer replied, 'Alex Ferguson just found out that the club owners are planning to cut his budget, and he's all depressed. He's stopped his car in the middle of the road and he's threatening to douse himself in petrol and set himself on fire. He says everybody hates him and he doesn't have any more money since he paid for Wayne Rooney's new contract. I'm walking around taking up a collection for him.'

'Oh, really? How much have you got so far?'

'Well, people are still siphoning, but right now I'd say about 300 gallons.'

3

THANK YOU FOR THE MUSIC

'One Song, we've only got one Song!'

Arsenal fans to Alexandre Song

Chants have always provided football fans with an opportunity to show their wit. At the end of the 2007–08 season when Manchester City fans heard that their Thai owner, Thaksin Shinawatra, planned to sack their boss Sven-Göran Eriksson, they chanted, to the tune of the Pink Floyd classic 'Another Brick in the Wall':

> We don't want no Phil Scolari,
> We don't need no Mourinho.
> Hey, Thaksin, leave our Sven alone!

The players responded to this touching show of loyalty by losing 8–1 to Middlesbrough. Earlier in the season, however, City had given their fans something to smile about when they shocked Manchester United to take a 2–0 lead at Old Trafford. As the United players made their weary way down the tunnel to face Sir Alex's hairdryer treatment, the City fans chorused to the tune of 'La donna è mobile':

> Time for your bollocking,
> Time for your bollocking.

Chants are often topical though they can sometimes be as tasteful as a Manchester United Christmas party. After Fulham owner Mohamed Al Fayed launched a stinging attack on the Duke of Edinburgh at the Princess Diana inquest, West Ham fans visiting Craven Cottage sang: 'There's only one Prince Philip.'

When Newcastle's sponsors Northern Rock went into crisis, visiting Derby fans sang:

> Banked with the Woolwich
> You should have banked with the Woolwich
> Banked with the Woolwich.

And after Victoria Beckham told Johnny Vaughan on *The Big Breakfast* that David liked to wear her knickers, and more specifically her thongs, opposing fans at Old Trafford chanted to the tune of 'Jesus Christ Superstar':

> David Beckham, Superstar,
> Wears Posh's knickers
> And a push-up bra.

Political correctness is seldom a feature of these chants. Take Liverpool fans on Wayne Rooney:

> He's fat,
> He's Scouse,
> He's going to rob your house.

Of course some chants are even affectionate, like the Kop's 2006 favourite:

> He's big, he's red, his feet hang out his bed,
> Peter Crouch, Peter Crouch!

Less kindly, West Ham fans serenaded Bobby Zamora to the tune of 'That's Amore':

When you're sat in row Z
And the ball hits your head
That's Zamora.

West Ham fans showed their ability to give a nice welcome to
a former favourite when Paul Ince took his Blackburn Rovers
to Upton Park: 'You're just a fat Eddie Murphy.' Then there
were the Colchester fans to their friends from the country, i.e.
Norwich fans: 'Does your livestock know you're here?' West
Ham fans, meanwhile, enquire of Fulham supporters, 'Does
your butler know you're here?'
    Some chants are designed simply to intimidate, like 'We've
got Dennis Bergkamp,' from the glory days of Wenger's
Arsenal. Some are downright triumphalist, like this one from
Chelsea fans flaunting their wealth:

Debt-free, wherever we may be,
We're going to buy everyone we see
And we don't give a f*** about the transfer fee,
'Cause we are the wealthy CFC.

Any selection of the best football chants must be a highly
subjective exercise, but the following is offered for
consideration as a possible top ten.

1

Early in the noughties, Leeds United seemed to be the ones
to watch, with a young manager in David O'Leary, a young
team and a Champions League semi-final place in 2001.
    Then it all went horribly wrong. The club had run up
huge debts, counting on a place in the Champions League
the following season to bring in revenue, a place that wasn't
achieved. Financial turmoil ensued and Rio Ferdinand, Leeds'
star player, was sold. The man the fans blamed was chairman
Peter Ridsdale. His last throw of the dice was to bring in Terry
Venables as manager, but he was not the footballing Moses
who would lead them into the Promised Land, and in fact
Leeds wandered further into the wilderness.

A new song, sung to the tune of Queen's 'Bohemian Rhapsody', was born: 'Bohemian Ridsdale':

> El Tel, just sold a man,
> Put a price tag on his head,
> Accepted an offer, now he's fled.
> El Tel, life had just begun,
> But now I've gone and thrown it all away.
> El Tel, oo-oo-oo-ooh,
> Didn't mean to let them buy,
> If I'm not back again this time tomorrow,
> Carry on, carry on, the whole team's now in tatters.
>
> Too late, 'Ridsdale Out' signs have come.
> Try to sell the team's main spine,
> Fans are booing all the time.
> Goodbye, everybody, I've got to go,
> Gotta leave you all behind to face the shit.
> Mama, oo-oo-oo-ooh,
> The fans want me to die
> They sometimes wish I wasn't on the board at all.

2

Some clubs' anthems, like Liverpool's 'You'll Never Walk Alone' or Manchester City's 'Blue Moon', approach the status of hymns. Perhaps the best example, though, is Sheffield United's paean to the joys of the Steel City, 'The Greasy Chip Butty Song', sung to the tune of John Denver's 'Annie's Song':

> You fill up my senses
> Like a gallon of Magnet,
> Like a packet of Woodbines,
> Like a good pinch of snuff,
> Like a night out in Sheffield,
> Like a greasy chip butty,
> Like Sheffield United,
> Come thrill me again

3

If brevity is the soul of wit, Chelsea fans struck gold with their chant for local rivals Fulham:

> He's fat, he's round,
> He's sold your f***ing ground,
> Al Fayed, Al Fayed!

4

Arsenal fans have scored with their tribute to Monsieur Petit:

> He's blond, he's slick,
> His name's a porno flick,
> Emmanuel, Emmanuel!

5

Liverpool fans sang a hymn of praise to Jamie Carragher's dad when he was temporarily banned from away matches after being arrested on suspicion of trying to enter a sports arena while drunk:

> He's red, he's sound,
> He's banned from every ground,
> Carra's dad, Carra's dad!

6

West Ham fans, singing to the tune of 'Daydream Believer', put the boot into Leeds' manager to considerable effect:

> Cheer up, Peter Reid.
> Oh, what can it mean?
> He sent Sunderland down
> And now he's trying with Leeds.

7

Manchester City and later Sunderland fans immortalised an item of clothing:

> Niall Quinn's disco pants are the best,
> They go up from his arse to his chest,
> They're better than Adam and the Ants,
> Niall Quinn's disco pants!

8

Manchester United fans used to celebrate the Neville brothers to the tune of David Bowie's 'Rebel Rebel':

> Neville Neville,
> They play in defence,
> Neville Neville,
> Their future's immense,
> Neville Neville,
> Like Jacko they're bad,
> Neville Neville
> Is the name of their dad.

9

Hospitable Manchester United fans greet their Liverpool counterparts with the following charming song about their Korean star Park Ji-Sung, to the tune of 'The Lord of the Dance':

> Park, Park, wherever you may be,
> You eat dogs in your home country.
> But it could be worse,
> You could be Scouse,
> Eating rats in your council house.

10

Arsenal fans were less than sympathetic to their visitors Spurs
after the Tottenham team were struck down by a tummy bug
after an Italian meal in a hotel in 2006:

> Lasagne, whoah! Lasagne, whoah!
> We laughed ourselves to bits
> When Tottenham had the shits.

PICK OF THE POPS

Some football songs seem to have been around for ever, with
the oldest still in use believed to be quaint Norwich City
favourite 'On the Ball, City', which has been sung for more
than a century:

> Kick it off, throw it in, have a little scrimmage,
> Keep it low, a splendid rush. Bravo! Win or die!
> On the ball, City, never mind the danger,
> Steady on, now's your chance.
> Hurrah! We've scored a goal!

Other chants, however, are bang up to date, with fans adapting
the lyrics of newly released hits. Take the version of the Kaiser
Chiefs' 'Oh My God' sung by Leeds fans, for example: 'Oh my
God, I can't believe it, we've never been this good away from
home!' In 2007, Colchester fans serenaded rivals Southend
to the tune of recent hit 'Monster' by The Automatic: 'What's
that coming over the hill? It's relegation, it's relegation!'
Appreciative Blackburn fans, meanwhile, have their own take
on Rihanna's 'Umbrella': 'There's only one Vince Grella, ella,
ella, hey, hey, hey.'

Sometimes the supporters delve deeper into pop history
for an appropriate tune. After a number of mistakes and an
own goal that gave Burnley a 1–0 win over Liverpool in the
2004–05 FA Cup, the Reds' fans were disillusioned with Djimi
Traoré and came up with a song to the tune of the Jackson
Five's 'Blame It on the Boogie':

Don't blame it on the Biscan,
Don't blame it on the Hamann,
Don't blame it on the Finnan,
Blame it on Traoré.
He just can't, he just can't, he just can't control his feet.

4

SIMPLY THE BEST

*'I spent a lot of my money on booze, birds and fast cars.
The rest I just squandered.'*

George Best

As the newspaper editor in John Ford's *The Man Who Shot Liberty Valance* says, 'When the legend becomes fact, print the legend.' To no sports figure has this adage been more often applied than to George Best.

In a 1991 interview on RTÉ television, with that characteristic mischievous glint in his eye, Best denied two apocryphal stories that had been told about him. The first was that he once said of a former Manchester United player, 'He couldn't pass wind.' The second was that he spent months chasing a girl because he overheard two men describing her as having loose morals. In fact, what one, a dentist, had said was that she had loose molars!

THE YOUNG ONES

In 1961, two fifteen year olds, Eric McMordie and George Best, set sail from Belfast for Liverpool for a two-week trial period with Manchester United. When they got to Manchester, they asked a cab driver to take them to Old Trafford. They were stunned when he replied, 'Which Old Trafford?' They had no idea that Old Trafford was also the name of a cricket ground. The trip to Manchester was a culture shock to Best, not least because it was the first time he'd ever worn long trousers.

WE MEET AGAIN

Best made his debut for United's reserve team in 1962 against West Brom. His immediate opponent was Brom's regular full-back, Welsh international Graham Williams, a tough player with an imposing physical presence. A year later, Best made his full debut, also against West Brom, and again his marker was Williams. United won 1–0 and Best earned good reviews for his performance. A few months later, Best made his debut for Northern Ireland against Wales, and again he was playing against Williams. The Irish won 3–2 with Best having two 'assists'. After the game, Williams made a dash for Best in the players' lounge.

'Will you stand still for a minute so I can look at your face?' he demanded.

'Why?' asked Best.

'Because all I've ever seen of you is your arse disappearing down the touchline.'

ROUGH STUFF

Inevitably, given his skill, Best was persistently targeted by the hard men of the game, but such was his speed that he seldom gave them the chance to clatter him. Attempts to psych Best out as he took to the field were a recurring feature of United's matches. One defender who had a reputation as a robust tackler came over to the United star before a match began and said, 'Don't look so worried, George. I'm in a humane mood today. I've put iodine on my studs.'

THE END OF THE WORLD AS WE KNOW IT

Best's importance to the United side is revealed in the old story of a staff member at the club who was informed by a colleague, 'I have terrible news for you.'

'What?'

'I'm afraid your wife is having an affair.'

'Is that all? I thought you were going to tell me that George Best was injured.'

MONEY TALKS

In his book *The Best of Times*, George looked back on some of his humorous experiences. He recalled that during the '60s, he was one of a group of players at United who felt that they deserved a pay increase. According to George, they decided to delegate Denis Law to negotiate with the manager on their behalf. Law went to speak to Matt Busby man to man while his colleagues waited with bated breath. They expected a protracted mediation, but Law returned within minutes. To their disappointment, he reported that the news was bad: Busby had pleaded poverty and he had been lucky to get five pounds out of him. The only consolation his fellow players could find was that it was better than nothing. At the end of the week, the players found that not only had their pay not increased, it had actually decreased. Mustering all the indignation they could manage, the players complained bitterly to their manager. Busby calmly replied, 'Take it up with Denis. When he came to me looking for a pay rise, I let him know how tight we are for money just now and persuaded him to accept a wage cut of five pounds a man to help the club out.'

By his own account, Best had some memorable exchanges with Law. One came when 'the Lawman' was complaining about the people from the Inland Revenue.

'I've had a final demand from the tax people. Eight hundred and fifty frigging quid. But I wrote them a letter.'

Best: 'Saying what?'

Law: 'Saying I couldn't remember borrowing it from them!'

After he retired from football, Law brought his unique verbal style to the world of punditry, scoring with insights like: 'Whoever wins today will win the championship no matter who wins,' and 'It's one of those goals that's invariably a goal.' When asked by Dickie Davies on one occasion, 'What's he going to be telling his team at half-time, Denis?' he replied, 'He'll be telling them that there are 45 minutes left to play.'

THE FIFTH BEATLE

A hero for his role in rescuing people after the Munich crash, Harry Gregg showed great skill and bravery in the 1966 European Cup quarter-final when United defeated Benfica 5–1 in the away leg. George Best had one of his finest games ever for United, scoring two goals. After the game, the Portuguese fans started shouting 'El Beatle' at him because his hairstyle was so similar to the Fab Four's. One fan, though, charged at him waving a butcher's knife. According to Best, Gregg rushed to his teammate's defence and wrestled the knife from him. The police were quickly on hand, but when they interrogated the fan they discovered that all he wanted was a lock of Best's hair!

HEALING HANDS

Best was noted for his womanising, once commenting of the young Gazza, 'They say Paul Gascoigne is the new George Best, but has he shagged three Miss Worlds?'

His attractiveness to the opposite sex was brilliantly illustrated by a story he told about a trip he took to the hospital following an injury sustained during a match. A nurse showed him to a cubicle and told him to take off his clothes and that she would examine him in a minute. As he turned around to take off his clothes, Best asked where he should leave them. The nurse replied, 'On top of mine.' She was already totally naked.

Best was able to joke about the impact that superstardom had on his game, once declaring, 'If I had been born ugly you would never have heard of Pelé.' He also had a good line about his capacity for excess: 'In 1969, I gave up women and alcohol. It was the worst 20 minutes of my life.'

ON THE UP

After his retirement, Best became a regular on the after-dinner speaking circuit, and one of the stories he used to tell was about the Amish boy and his father who were visiting a mall. They were amazed by almost everything they saw, but especially by two shiny, silver walls that moved apart and back together again.

The boy asked, 'What is this?'

The father responded, 'Son, I have never seen anything like this in my life. I don't know what it is.'

While the boy and his father were watching wide-eyed, an old lady in a wheelchair rolled up to the moving walls and pressed a button. The walls opened and the lady rolled between them into a small room. The walls closed and the boy and his father watched small, numbered circles above the walls light up. They continued to watch as the circles lit up again in reverse order. The walls opened up again and a beautiful young woman stepped out.

The father said to his son, 'Go get your mother.'

RISE AND SHINE

During his days with Fulham, Best was rooming with Rodney Marsh while they were on tour. Marsh recalls that Best went out on the town even though the team were to get a 10 a.m. flight the next morning. When George came into the hotel and asked for a wake-up call, the concierge said, 'Certainly, Mr Best. What time?'

George said, 'Seven thirty.'

The concierge replied, 'It's twenty to eight now!'

CONFUSION

During his hell-raising days, apocryphal stories of Best's nights out abounded. One had it that towards the end of an evening, Best was at the bar when he spotted someone he recognised from back home. He rushed up and greeted his 'friend' effusively.

'What brings you to London?' George asked.

'I live here,' was the reply, in a tone that had Best been less inebriated would have told him that the man had never met him before.

'Didn't you used to have a beard at one time?' asked Best.

'No.'

'You used to be taller. You must have shrunk. But it's great to see you all the same, Sam.'

'My name isn't Sam, it's Cliff.'

'Good God! You've changed your name as well?'

DOCTOR'S ORDERS

In 2002, Best was critically ill and needed major surgery, which required him to receive a lot of blood. Afterwards, when a journalist asked Best how much blood he had required, George quipped, 'I was in for ten hours and had forty pints – beating my previous record by twenty minutes.'

Best's battle with alcohol addiction resulted in his appearance drunk on Terry Wogan's live chat show in 1990. It was not the stuff of good public relations and led one journalist to describe him as 'George Best, a legend in his own stupor'.

Best used to joke that his wild friends Oliver Reed and Alex Higgins had rung him up afterwards and said, 'We don't know what all the fuss is about, George. You looked fine to us.'

IN THE MOVIES

Best's story was, not surprisingly, turned into a film. Sky Sports' George Gavin seemed to struggle with the concept when he interviewed one of the actors and asked, 'So, this movie you star in, the life story of George Best – tell us what it's about.'

BEST WIT

One of the traits that is often forgotten in assessments of Best is his wit. He once took the wind out of a reporter's sails by answering a prying question in the following way: 'If you want the secret of my success with women, then don't smoke, don't take drugs and don't be too particular.'

He also caught his United colleague Martin Buchan on the hop when he complimented Best on his new coat: 'From the style, it looks French.'

Best's reply was, 'It is from France. It's Toulon and Toulouse.'

His humour was often self-deprecating and he could laugh even at the darker side of his life. When asked why he'd gone to play for Vancouver Whitecaps, he answered, 'Because I saw an advert on the side of a London bus inviting me to "Drink Canada Dry",' and on accepting the Footballer of the Century award in 1999, he began his speech, 'It's a pleasure to be standing up here. It's a pleasure to be standing up.'

5

KING KEV

'There will be no siestas in Madrid tonight.'

Kevin Keegan

A newspaper is rather caustically defined by George Bernard Shaw as a device 'unable to distinguish between a bicycle accident and the collapse of civilisation'. It is no surprise, then, that the media have had a field day with the eventful career of Kevin Keegan. They've also got a lot of mileage out of his often mystifying pronouncements.

FROM THE HORSE'S MOUTH

Keegan is a national treasure and a national resource. Nobody has produced more natural gas than Kevin, as my top 40 proves:

1. 'I am reluctant to tell you all I know as I really do not know anything.'

On Dennis Wise's appointment as director of football at Newcastle

2. 'The only way we will get into Europe is by ferry.'

Following his second coming at Newcastle

3. 'Over a season, you'll get goals disallowed that are good and you'll get goals that are good disallowed.'

4.   'Bobby Robson must be thinking of throwing some fresh legs on.'

5.   'I'll never play at Wembley again, unless I play at Wembley again.'

6.   'It's like a toaster, the ref's shirt pocket. Every time there's a tackle, up pops a yellow card.'

7.   'Gary [Lineker] always weighed up his options, especially when he had no choice.'

8.   'Goalkeepers today aren't born until they're in their late 20s or 30s.'

9.   'I don't think there is anybody bigger or smaller than Maradona.'

10. 'They compare Steve McManaman to Steve Heighway and he's nothing like him, but I can see why – it's because he's a bit different.'

11. 'Sometimes there are too many generals and not enough, er, people waving to the generals as they, er, walk past.'

12. 'That would have been a goal if it wasn't saved.'

Unlucky 13.
     'There's only one team going to win it now, and that's England.'

*During a 1998 World Cup match, just before
Dan Petrescu scored Romania's winner*

14. 'The ref was vertically 15 yards away.'

15. 'In some ways, cramp is worse than having a broken leg.'

16. 'The 33 or 34 year olds will be 36 or 37 by the time the next World Cup comes around if they're not careful.'

17. 'Argentina won't be at Euro 2000 because they're from South America.'

18. 'Despite his white boots, he has real pace.'

19. 'They [Argentina] are the second best team in the world, and there's no higher praise than that.'

20. 'England have the best fans in the world and Scotland's fans are second to none.'

21. 'England can end the millennium as it started – as the greatest football nation in the world.'

22. 'You can't do better than go away from home and get a draw.'

23. 'He's using his strength. And that is his strength, his strength.'

24. 'The tide is very much in our court now.'

25. 'Chile have three options – they could win or lose.'

26. 'I came to Nantes two years ago and it's much the same today, except that it's totally different.'

27. 'I know what is around the corner – I just don't know where the corner is. But the onus is on us to perform and we must control the bandwagon.'

28. 'It's understandable that people are keeping one eye on the pot and another up the chimney.'

29. 'I'd love to be a mole on the wall in the Liverpool dressing-room at half-time.'

30. 'I never talk about Uriah Rennie except to say I don't like him as a referee.'

31. 'The substitute is about to come on. He's a player who was left out of the starting line-up today.'

32. 'Nicolas Anelka left Arsenal for £23 million and they built a training ground on him.'

33. 'I'm not trying to make excuses [for a David Seaman howler], but I think the lights may have been a problem.'

34. 'Hungary is very similar to Bulgaria. I know they're different countries . . .'

35. 'Life wouldn't be worth living if you could buy confidence, because the rich people would have it all and everybody else would . . . would have to make their own arrangements.'

36. 'You can't play with a one-armed goalkeeper . . . not at this level.'

37. 'You get bunches of players like you do bananas . . . though that is a bad comparison.'

38. 'You just need one or two players playing well to have a chance in this league. But you need nine or ten players playing well to have a chance to win.'

39. 'We don't get any marks for effort like in ice skating.'

40. 'Richard Dunne has always been in the frame. When he has been out of the frame, he took himself out of it for one reason or another.'

ALWAYS LOOK ON THE BRIGHT SIDE OF LIFE

Keegan is known for his boundless optimism, and perhaps he's got good reason for it, especially if Jack Charlton is to be believed. 'If Kevin Keegan fell into the Tyne,' says Big Jack, 'he'd come up with a salmon in his mouth.' With the notable exception of the time he lost his temper and began ranting about Alex Ferguson and Man United on live television ('I will love it if we beat them! Love it!'), Keegan is known as one of the game's nice guys. Perhaps that explains Duncan McKenzie's observation: 'He is the Julie Andrews of football.'

MISSED OPPORTUNITIES

At training one day, Keegan is less than impressed by a fringe player with his team, and says to him, 'It's a pity you didn't take up the game sooner.'

'You mean because I'd be better now?'

'No, I mean you would have given it up long ago.'

A GOOD WALK SPOILED

Kevin Keegan is one of a strange breed who can drive seventy miles an hour in heavy traffic with perfect ease but blow up on a two-foot putt if somebody coughs. Yes, he's a keen golfer. So keen, in fact, that following his retirement as a player he spent some seven years in Marbella working on his handicap and has been quoted as saying, 'The day I don't get emotional about football, I'll be back playing golf again in Spain.'

On a holiday to America, Kevin Keegan meets Stevie Wonder in a bar. Keegan tells him about the joys of football and in return Stevie fills him in on all the music greats like Michael Jackson. Stevie casually mentions to Keegan that he plays golf. When Keegan expresses surprise, he tells him that he's been playing for years.

'But how can you play golf?' Keegan asks.

'I get my caddie to stand in the middle of the fairway and call to me. I listen for the sound of his voice and play the ball towards him, then when I get to where the ball lands, the caddie moves to the green or further down the fairway and again I play the ball toward his voice,' explains Stevie.

'But how do you putt?' Keegan wonders.

'Well,' says Stevie, 'I get my caddie to lean down in front of the hole and call to me with his head on the ground, and I just play the ball to the sound of his voice.'

Keegan is incredulous and says to Stevie, 'We must play a game some time.'

Stevie replies, 'Well, people don't take me seriously, so I only play for money, and I never play for less than $1,000 a hole.'

Keegan thinks it over and says, 'OK, I'm up for that. When would you like to play?'

'I don't care – any night next week is OK with me.'

In an effort to improve his golf game, Keegan goes for a lesson and makes the mistake of asking, 'Should I bend my knees more?' The pro replies, 'Yes and pray, brother, pray!'

Keegan is playing with a friend one day when his partner says, 'Did you hear about Bill?'

'No,' replies Kevin curiously, 'what about him?'

'He went mad last week and beat his wife to death with a golf club.'

Keegan shudders. 'God, that's awful.'

They pause for a moment's reflection, and then Kevin asks, 'How many strokes?'

Keegan is playing a round of golf when his drive lands on an anthill. Rather than move the ball, he decides to hit it where it lies. He takes a mighty swing. Clouds of dirt, sand and ants explode from the spot – everything, that is, but the golf ball. Keegan lines up and tries another shot. Again, clouds of dirt, sand and ants go flying, but the golf ball doesn't even wiggle.

Two ants survive this onslaught. One dazed ant says to the other, 'What are we going to do?'

The other replies, 'I don't know about you, but I'm going to get on the ball.'

6

THE GAFFER

'Who wants to be a football manager? Well, people like me who are too old to play, too poor to be a director and too much in love with the game to be an agent.'

Steve Coppell

Managers bring great joy to fans – sometimes when they arrive at a club but more often when they leave. This chapter celebrates the many managers who prove the truth of Jimmy Greaves' famous catchphrase: 'It's a funny old game.'

MEDICAL MATTERS

A medical professor had just finished a lecture on the subject of mental health and started to ask questions of the first-year students. He asked, 'How would you diagnose a patient who walks back and forth screaming at the top of his lungs one minute, then sits in a chair weeping uncontrollably the next?'

One bright young student piped up, 'A Premiership football manager?'

LOADS OF MONEY

On the plus side, Premier League managers are very well paid. When asked in 2003 about his role as Portsmouth's manager,

Harry Redknapp replied with commendable honesty. 'Why did I take the job? Skint.'

NEW DIRECTION

After his tenure as England manager ended in ignominy in 2007, Steve McClaren must have been feeling down, especially when he read the *Daily Mail*'s verdict: 'Great leaders inspire their men to glory. Steve McClaren will be remembered as a wally with a brolly.'

He was badly in need of some good PR, but at least he could take comfort in the fact that even some of those 'great leaders' the *Mail* was talking about would have trouble in today's job market.

JULIUS CAESAR: 'My last job involved a lot of office politics and back-stabbing. I'd like to get away from all that.'

JESSE JAMES: 'I can list among my experiences and skills leadership, extensive travel, logistical organisation, an intimate understanding of firearms and a knowledge of security measures at numerous banks.'

MARIE ANTOINETTE: 'My management style has been criticised, but I'd like to think of myself as a people person.'

HAMLET: 'My position was eliminated in a hostile takeover.'

GENGHIS KHAN: 'My primary talent is downsizing. In my last job I downsized my staff, my organisation and the population of several countries.'

BURDENSOME

During his time as England manager, Steve McClaren is sitting beside a boy on a long plane journey. As there's no film and he hasn't got a book with him, McClaren asks the boy if he'd be interested in having a chat with him about the national team.

'OK,' says the boy, 'that could be interesting. But let me ask you a question first. A horse, a cow and a deer all eat grass. The same stuff. Yet a deer excretes little pellets, while a cow turns out flat pats and a horse produces clumps of dried grass. Why do you think that is?'

'Hmmm,' says Steve. 'I have no idea.'

'Well, then,' says the boy, 'how is it you get to decide who plays for the country when you don't know shit?'

HARRY'S GAME

McClaren, of course, was replaced by Fabio Capello. Capello's biggest fan is not Harry Redknapp. Commenting on Capello's choice of tactical formation in 2008, Harry remarked: 'The last time I heard of 3–2–1 was that show with Ted Rodgers and Dusty Bin.'

Mind you, Harry's own tactical nous is not the eighth wonder of the world. His technical advice to Roman Pavlyuchenko from the Tottenham dugout was nothing if not forthright. Apparently, he directed the Russian interpreter to 'tell him to just f***ing run about'.

METAPHORICALLY SPEAKING

Ian Holloway, current manager of Blackpool, formerly of QPR, Plymouth Argyle and Leicester City, tends to be less direct, rarely missing an opportunity for a tortured metaphor:

'Paul Furlong is my vintage Rolls-Royce and he cost me nothing. We polish him, look after him and I have him fine-tuned by my mechanics. We take good care of him because we have to drive him every day, not just save him for weddings.'

On the QPR striker

'It's like the film *Men in Black*. I walk around in a black suit, white shirt and black tie . . . I've had to flash my white light every now and again to erase some memories, but I feel we've got hold of the galaxy now. It's in our hands.'

On life at QPR

'I always say that scoring goals is like driving a car. When the striker is going for goal, he's pushing down that accelerator, so the rest of the team has to come down off that clutch. If the clutch and the accelerator are down at the same time, then you're going to have an accident.'

'It's all very well having a great pianist playing but it's no good if you haven't got anyone to get the piano on the stage in the first place, otherwise the pianist would be standing there with no bloody piano to play.'

Responding to those who had criticised him
for using defensive players in midfield

Even when he goes for tried and tested phrases, he mixes it up a bit to keep it interesting:

'There was a spell in the second half when I took my heart off my sleeve and put it in my mouth.'

'Every dog has its day, and today is woof day!'

Having secured promotion for QPR, 2004

HOLLOWAY HOWLERS

Yes, Holloway has certainly made some interesting comments down the years. My 'famous five' Hollowayisms are:

1. 'Right now everything is going wrong for me. If I fell in a barrel of boobs, I'd come out sucking my thumb.'

2. 'I couldn't be more chuffed if I were a badger at the start of the mating season.'

Holloway savours a QPR victory

3. 'The referee is from my neck of the woods, and down there people say there's one in every village.'

4. 'I feel like I have been acting in *Coronation Street* all of my life and now I am King Lear.'

   On leaving Plymouth to become manager of Leicester in 2007

5. 'I had a midfield so young they should have been in nappies.'

   After Leicester lost to Southampton in the 2008 FA Cup

ICY CONDITIONS

Holloway succeeded Gerry Francis as QPR manager. Francis was very unlucky at Loftus Road, and in 1991, during a severe injury crisis, he commented, 'There's more ice down there than sunk the *Bismarck*.'

SHANKS

One of the great managerial wits was the man who made Liverpool the force they were in the 1970s, Bill Shankly. His impact on the club was revealed in the comment of a depressed Liverpool fan frustrated by the team's failure to challenge for the Premier League again in 2008: 'If Bill Shankly was alive today, he'd be turning in his grave.'

In 1951, Shankly was managing Third Division Carlisle United, who pulled off a shock 0–0 draw at mighty Arsenal in the FA Cup. When the aristocrats arrived at Brunton Park for the replay, Shankly burst into his side's dressing-room to announce with a flourish, 'Boys, I've just seen them getting out of their coach. They should be in hospital. They're in a right state.' Arsenal won 4–1, but afterwards Shankly told his team, 'Boys, you've just lost to the greatest side in England – but it took them two games.' It was a tactic he was to employ throughout his managerial career: build your players up, make them feel great, and if you have to criticise them, do so in private. His philosophy was: 'I don't drop players – I make changes.'

Shankly's dry wit was most evident in his comments about the club's bitter rivals Everton. When Alan Ball left Blackpool for Everton, Shankly called him up and said, 'Congratulations on your move, son. You'll be playing near a great side.'

His take on the pre-match chat between Princess Margaret and Everton captain Brian Labone at the 1966 FA Cup final was as follows.

HRH: 'Mr Labone, where is Everton?'

Labone: 'In Liverpool, Ma'am.'

HRH: 'Of course, we had your first team here last year.'

Shanks never missed an opportunity to play up the rivalry, commenting, 'When I've got nothing better to do, I look down the league table to see how Everton are getting along.' He claimed, 'If Everton were playing down at the bottom of my garden, I'd draw the curtains,' and maintained, 'This city has two great teams – Liverpool and Liverpool reserves.'

He could be just as funny about players. Asked his opinion on the young Mick Channon, who was making a name for himself at Southampton in the late '60s, Shanks replied that he was very good. The reporter pushed him further and asked, 'Is he as good a player as Stanley Matthews?'

'Oh, aye,' said Shankly, 'he's as good a player as Stan. But what you have to remember is that Stan is 65 now!'

On one occasion, when he was discussing a much sought-after star player of the day with fellow manager Tommy Docherty, Docherty remarked, 'A hundred thousand wouldn't buy him,' to which Shankly responded, 'I know, and I'm one of them.'

Shanks's waspish wit was also evident in his comment on former Spurs forward Martin Chivers: 'The big boy is deceptive. He's slower than he looks.'

What is taken to the FA Cup final every year but never used? The correct answer is the losing team's ribbons for the trophy, but in the 1970s Shankly suggested the answer was Malcolm MacDonald following his ineffectual performances for both Newcastle and Arsenal in that fixture.

In the dressing-room, Shanks didn't spare his own players. He told Tommy Smith, 'You, Smithy, you could start a riot in a graveyard,' and when goalie Ray Clemence apologised for a mistake, admitting that he should have kept his legs together, Shankly responded, 'Wrong. It's your mother who should have!'

BOB'S BUILDING JOB

Shanks was replaced by Bob Paisley as Liverpool manager. He was a wonderful manager but not the clearest of speakers. Before his first match in charge, he gave a passionate speech. Afterwards, one player supposedly commented, 'I didn't understand a bloody word he said, but it sounded pretty impressive.'

Like Shankly, Paisley was extremely proud of the club, on one occasion commenting, 'Mind, I've been here during the bad times too. One year we came second.'

DOOM AND GLOOM

Managers have a great capacity to see the glass as half-full or half-empty depending on what suits them. It's usually half-empty, and the following are my top ten managerial whinges:

1. 'Even the chef has been out for two weeks with a hernia.'

West Ham boss Alan Curbishley
bemoans the club's injury crisis in 2008

2. 'I've got more points on my licence. I'm not joking.'

Paul Jewell's verdict on his Derby team's dismal league
performance in 2007–08

3. 'Marriages struggle to survive this job. Your sanity is under threat. You wonder whether some will actually escape with their lives.'

David Pleat, in the hot seat at Sheffield Wednesday

4. 'The way Ashley Young is built, he looks like a heavy shower could kill him.'

Martin O'Neill worries about his Aston Villa winger

5. 'England have to play like England. But maybe a little bit better.'

Franco Baldini, Fabio Capello's assistant

6. 'Rather than making any comment, I'd like to talk to the player first. But he let us down badly.'

Bray Wanderers manager Pat Devlin reacts to Wesley Charles's dismissal against St Pats

7. 'There's a financial problem and there's no money either.'

Gerry Francis after being appointed manager of QPR for the second time

8. 'The first thing that went wrong was half-time. We could have done without that.'

Graham Taylor explaining England's second-half collapse against Sweden in the European Championships in 1992

9. 'A lot of hard work went into this defeat.'

Malcolm Allison

10. 'With our luck, one of our players must be bonking a witch.'

Ken Brown, manager at Norwich City

SICK AS A PARROT

Nicknames are an important part of football culture. Gary Megson became known as 'Suitcase' during his playing days because he was never at one club for long. During his stay at Sheffield Wednesday, Megson played alongside Paul Hart, who supposedly had two nicknames: 'Fossil' and 'Horlicks'. He was known as 'Fossil' because of his lived-in looks and 'Horlicks' because his conversation had the same effect on people as the bedtime drink.

Megson's stay at Nottingham Forest was particularly short. According to George Best in his book *The Best of Times*, Megson had a habit of making himself sick before a match and at half-time. He was making his Forest debut in a friendly game with Dundee when Forest's manager, Brian Clough, came into the dressing-room and heard retching noises coming from the toilets.

'What the hell is that noise?' he asked.

'It's Meggy being sick,' replied one of the players.

Clough called Megson back into the room, and demanded, 'Why are you being sick?'

'I'm always sick at half-time.'

'Not in my dressing-room you're not.'

Megson never played for Clough again. His first-team career with Forest lasted one match.

STRANGE BUT TRUE

Brian Clough had some unusual motivational strategies. During a reserves match he was not very happy with Forest's strikers, especially Nigel Jemson, who, like Megson, did not have a long stay with the club. Things had not gone well for Forest in the first half. At half-time, all the team were sitting in the dressing-room with their heads bowed low. Clough walked up to Jemson and forcefully instructed him to stand up. Jemson obediently complied with Clough's demand. 'Have you ever been hit in the stomach, son?' Cloughie enquired. As soon as Jemson had said no, Clough hit him hard in the midriff. Jemson doubled up in pain. 'Now you have, son,' said Clough calmly.

THE MAGNIFICENT SEVEN

Brian Clough gifted the football world a treasure trove of barbed comments and outspoken remarks. My seven deadly Cloughisms are:

1. 'Football hooligans? Well, there are 92 club chairmen for a start.'

2. 'Trevor Brooking floats like a butterfly and stings like one too.'

3. 'I can't even spell "spaghetti" never mind talk Italian. How could I tell an Italian to get the ball? He might grab mine.'

4. 'I'm ill-tempered, rude and wondering what's for tea: just the same as always.'

    Asked how he was on the afternoon following his retirement

5. 'Very few players have the courage of my convictions.'

6. 'When you get to a certain age, there's no coming back. I've decided to pick my moment to quit very carefully – in about 200 years' time.'

7. 'That Seaman is a handsome young man, but he spends too much time looking in his mirror rather than at the ball. You can't keep goal with hair like that.'

THE BURN(S)ING ISSUES

When Forest won consecutive European Cups in 1979 and 1980, their centre-half was Kenny Burns. Clough warned Kenny many times about passing the ball square across the front of his own goal. During the second half of a big match, he again defied Clough's orders and repeated the feat. The final whistle blew and Burns walked back to the dressing-room to find an envelope waiting for him at his changing place. He opened it. It was a typed letter on official club paper – he had been fined by the manager for disobeying orders.

RAISING THE STAKES

During the late 1970s, Larry Lloyd was Forest's centre-half. Forest had played a match in Greece and the team were congregating in the hotel foyer before departing for the airport. Although the temperature was soaring, the manager had decreed that everybody was to report wearing the club blazer and slacks. The only rebel who did not conform was Lloyd, who was wearing a tracksuit.

Clough shouted over, 'Go and get your blazer on!'

Lloyd was having none of it: 'No, it's too warm. I'm wearing my tracksuit.'

The manager replied, 'If you don't put it on, I will fine you £100.'

The answer was immediate: 'I don't care.'

'Right, that's £100. If you don't put it on now, I'll double it.'

'Go on, then.'

And so it went on and on.

During the trip back, the fine was doubled many times over, until Larry reached home having lost about six months' wages.

Lloyd had won three England caps at Liverpool but fell out of the international reckoning until he joined Forest. On his recall to the heart of the English defence, England were thrashed 4–1 by Wales. Not long afterwards, Larry was confronted by Clough in the Forest dressing-room. 'Larry,' he asked, 'which England international got two caps on the same day?'

'I don't know, boss. Who was it?'

'You did. Your fourth and your last!'

Evidently, Clough was not renowned for his diplomacy, so it probably came as no great surprise to the interviewer who asked his opinion of sports minister Colin Moynihan when he replied, 'Have you ever seen anybody like him in your bloody life? I'd like to grab him by the balls and strangle him.'

AFTERNOON TEA

At Forest, Clough was the uncrowned king. Despite his earlier successes with Derby, he was not always treated with such reverence at the Baseball Ground. One day, he rang down to the dressing-room for a cup of tea. The apprentice who answered said simply, 'Bugger off,' and slammed down the phone.

Clough rang down again, asking, 'Do you know who I am?'

The apprentice answered with another question: 'Do you know who I am?'

'No.'

'Well, bugger off again, then.'

BARMY BOSSES

Clough was not by any means the only football manager with a flair for words, as the following selection of managerial *bons mots* illustrates:

'Before the match, I told my players they will be playing against 11 guys ready to fight for each other for 90 minutes – not with each other!'

> *Spartak Moscow coach Oleg Romantsev after the infamous brawl involving Blackburn's Graeme Le Saux and David Batty*

'I'm not a believer in luck, although I do believe you need it.'

> *Alan Ball*

'I honestly believe that we can go all the way to Wembley . . . unless somebody knocks us out.'

> *Dave Bassett*

'I promise results, not promises.'

John Bond

'I would advise anyone coming to the match to come early and not leave until the end, otherwise they might miss something.'

John Toshack

'We could be putting the hammer in Luton's coffin.'

Ray Wilkins

'Apparently he was eating a lasagne and somehow pulled a hamstring. It has to be a world first.'

Coventry manager Micky Adams explaining how Andrew Whing injured himself in 2005

'What I said to them at half-time would be unprintable on the radio.'

Gerry Francis

'I must admit, when I came here I thought we were certs to finish bottom. Now I am very optimistic and I think we'll finish second bottom.'

Barry Fry reflecting on his move to Southend

'If you can't stand the heat in the dressing-room, get out of the kitchen.'

Terry Venables

'You weigh up the pros and cons and put them in chronological order.'

Dave Bassett

'We performed very well, but in the first action for them they scored. In our best moment they scored two goals. That would kill a bull, as we say in Italy.'

Claudio Ranieri

'The lads ran their socks into the ground.'

Sir Alex Ferguson

'If they [Manchester United] play well, they will win. If they don't play well, they will get a penalty and still win.'

José Mourinho, not even slightly bitter in 2007

'OK so we lost – but good things can come from it, negative and positive.'

Glenn Hoddle

'Our major problem is that we don't know how to play football.'

Sam Allardyce on Bolton in 2003

'Certain people are for me, certain people are pro me.'

Yes, everybody loves Terry Venables

'Like trying to push custard up a hill.'

Howard Wilkinson on Sunderland's relegation battle in 2003

IN THE HOT SEAT

Down the years, managers have also been the subject of some classic quotes.

'At least he's learning to speak more better English.'

Chelsea legend Ron 'Chopper' Harris on Claudio Ranieri

'All the Leeds United team are 100 per cent behind the manager, but I can't speak for the rest of the team.'

Brian Greenhoff

'He [Graham Taylor] should leave the same way he arrived: fired with enthusiasm.'

Joe Lovejoy, The Independent

'I don't mind Lawrie Sanchez spending £25 million of my money on players but in return I expect six points from the next two games. If I don't, I'm going to send round the biggest bouncer we've got at Harrods to hold him down and shove a pepper suppository up his arse.'

Mohamed Al Fayed offers a unique take on the dreaded vote of no confidence during an after-dinner speech

'Yes, I was surprised about George [Graham]'s sacking, but, as I always say, nothing surprises me in football.'

Les Ferdinand

'The nice aspect about football is that if things go wrong, it's the manager who gets the blame.'

Gary Lineker

'Even now, a team of linguists is at work translating Don Revie's writings on the game from the original gibberish into Arabic.'

Michael Parkinson

'It was just his presence – he didn't have any.'

There was no love lost between Gerry Taggart and Northern Ireland boss Lawrie McMenemy

'Matt [Busby] always believed Manchester United would be one of the greatest clubs in the world. He was the eternal optimist. In 1968, he still hoped Glenn Miller was just missing.'

Pat Crerand

FAST MOVER

In 2007, former Fulham and West Ham striker Leroy Rosenior was made manager of Torquay United. Ten minutes after the press conference to announce his appointment, the chairman told him that the club had been sold to a business consortium and that he was sacked. Rosenior joked, 'Obviously, they thought I had done a fantastic job after ten minutes.'

TOUGHER THAN THE REST

Football has always had its hard men, as Everton's manager Harry Catterick acknowledged in 1971 when he said, 'Every team has a clogger whose job it is to put a clever opponent out of the match.' When Joe Kinnear was manager of Wimbledon, he famously claimed, 'Psychology won't work on us – we have too many psychos in the side,' and Graeme Souness, with commendable honesty, once said of his playing days, 'If they had had video evidence in my day, I reckon I would still be doing time!'

Of course, football's not the only sport in which tough tackles and physical exchanges are to be expected. Rugby union was notoriously brutal in the 1970s, with the legendary Welsh coach Carwyn James coining the phrase 'get your retaliation in first' and England international Mike Burton devoting a chapter of his autobiography to the best punches he encountered in his career. Across the pond, the great sportswriter Red Smith once quipped, 'I went to a fight and an ice hockey match broke out.'

IT'S NOT OUR FAULT

Alex Ferguson is one of the many managers who have reacted badly to referees' decisions. Few, though, have gone as far as Ratsimandresy Ratsarazaka, manager of Madagascan side Stade Olympique de l'Emyrne. In 2002, when SOE were reigning champions, Ratsarazaka took severe exception to a decision the referee had made in the first half. At half-time, he instructed his side to keep kicking the ball into their own net and score as many own goals as possible. They lost 149–0. A comparable result in the Premiership would be for Sunderland to beat Arsenal 149–0 at the Emirates. It's safe to say that Arsène Wenger is unlikely ever to allow his players to be arsing around that much.

HALF-TIME TALK

One fiery football manager burst into the dressing-room as the second half of a game was about to begin. 'All right!' he roared. 'All of you lazy, no-good, thickheaded bastards – out on that field, now!'

All the players jumped to their feet and rushed off – except for a veteran defender, who was still sitting in the corner.

'Well?' roared the manager.

'Well,' he said, 'there certainly were a lot of them, weren't there?'

SERGEANT WILKO

In autumn 2002, after Ireland lost 4–2 to Russia and Mick McCarthy resigned as Ireland manager, the consensus was that McCarthy was a shoo-in to replace Peter Reid as manager of struggling Sunderland. To everyone's surprise, the job went to Howard Wilkinson, who was technical director at the FA at the time.

Mick aside, Wilkinson didn't have the stiffest competition for the job. One of the other applicants, as the club's website revealed, was a fan who offered two inducements: 'My spouse is willing to launder the football kits after each match and my uncle Jack, who has his own allotment and a petrol lawnmower, is willing to cut the grass once or even twice a week.'

Wilko is not particularly renowned for his sense of humour, but in his first week he showed a waspish streak. He was unhappy with the general level of fitness in the squad and particularly with that of Tore André Flo.

Wilkinson asked him, 'Have you got a boot sponsor?'

'Yes,' said Flo.

'Good. I'll get them to send you some lighter ones.'

TIME TO SAY GOODBYE

After a training session one day a number of years ago, a manager who shall remain nameless was surprised to receive a call from the club chairman. He was even more surprised when the chairman asked him if he'd ever thought about retirement.

'Good heavens, no,' said the manager.

'Well, I should if I were you,' said the chairman. 'I have to tell you that you're fired.'

HEART IN MOUTH

Football managers have generated, directly and indirectly, some strong feelings. The following is my top 20 of heartfelt comments, emotional outbursts and ill-thought-through pronouncements by and about managers.

1. 'Football management should carry a government health warning, like it does on a packet of fags.'

    Barry Fry, Peterborough manager

2. 'My mother told me there would be days like these. She just didn't tell me when and how many.'

    Mick McCarthy after Sunderland conceded a 94th-minute equaliser to West Brom when they were on the verge of an elusive victory

3. 'This is farcical that Sol has been cited. We must be living in farci-land.'

    Arsène Wenger, upset about the referral of a Sol Campbell tackle to the FA's video advisory committee

4. 'We did not deserve to lose today. We weren't beaten, we lost.'

    Sunderland's Howard Wilkinson

5. 'I can't change now. I'm like Frank Sinatra – I always do it my way. I told the players everything I did in the Monaco game was wrong. I changed things to win the match, but we lost and I was thinking, "Oh f***, Claudio, why, why? Bad Tinkerman!"'

    Claudio Ranieri wishes he'd left
    well enough alone at Chelsea

6. 'I'd never allow myself to let myself call myself a coward.'

    Graham Taylor has himself under control

7. 'Can you please tell us – what language is he speaking?'

    Enquiry from a Romanian television station after
    being sent a tape of a Gordon Strachan press conference

8. 'Glenn Roeder has stood up all his life and he will always stay standing up whatever happens to him.'

    Glenn Roeder's self-analysis

9. 'Most of our fans get behind us and are fantastic. But those who don't should shut the hell up or they can come round to my house and I will fight them.'

    Ian Holloway

10. 'I've got to play for a Frenchman? You've got to be joking.'

    Tony Adams remembers his reaction
    to Arsène Wenger's appointment

11. 'They have to concentrate not only when they have the ball or when their opponents have the ball but also when neither of them has the ball.'

    Graham Taylor

12. 'Glenn Roeder knows that they have to score more goals than they concede if they want to win the game.'

John Anderson reassures Newcastle fans that Glenn Roeder has what it takes to be manager of Newcastle

13. 'Glenn Roeder will think for a few minutes before making a rash decision.'

Steve Stone sounds less bullish about Roeder's stewardship of Newcastle

14. 'As one door closes, another one shuts.'

Howard Wilkinson

15. 'I wouldn't quote Kipling to the lads. They'd probably think I was talking about cakes.'

Leicester City manager Rob Kelly in 2006

16. 'We were undone by our Achilles heel, which has been stabbing us in the back all season.'

David O'Leary

17. 'I had to go. I felt like a turkey waiting for Christmas.'

Frank Clark on his departure from Nottingham Forest

18. 'I was left partly with a feeling of relief. I worked in Spain, and even the bull dies quicker than I did this summer.'

Same scenario, different animal for Howard Kendall at Everton

19. 'To me personally, it's nothing personal to me.'

Former England manager Ron Greenwood

20. 'We can't behave like crocodiles and cry over spilt milk and broken eggs.'

Giovanni Trapattoni isn't shedding any tears either

A POLICY CHANGE

A newly appointed Premiership manager was having open interviews for the position of office secretary.

'What's your name?' he asked the first man who showed up.

'John,' the applicant replied.

The manager scowled. 'Look, I don't know what kind of namby-pamby place you worked in before, but I don't call anyone by their first name. It breeds familiarity and that leads to a breakdown in authority. I refer to my employees by their last name only – Smith, Jones, etc. That's all. I am to be referred to only as 'boss'. Now that we've got that straight, what's your last name?'

The new man sighed. 'Darling. My name is John Darling.'

'OK, John, the next thing I want to tell you is . . .'

THE GOLDEN YEARS

In his later years, Matt Busby was occasionally asked to reflect on the ageing process. When a BBC journalist asked him how he felt about getting older and missing out on day-to-day involvement in management, he cited comedian George Burns' comment on turning 80: 'I can do all the things today I did at 18, which tells you how pathetic I was at 18.' On players getting older, Busby remarked to the former United defender and Ireland international Shay Brennan, 'You know whether a player is great coming to the end of his career. A great player when he is gone will never be forgotten. A bad player is one who is not yet gone but is already forgotten!'

NO KIDDING

While football managers often come out with baffling statements, there are times when they go too far the other way. Let's just say that they're not afraid to state the obvious.

'If you can get through the first round, you have a good chance of getting into the next one.'

Norwich's Nigel Worthington

'If history is going to repeat itself, I should think we can expect the same thing again.'

Terry Venables

'When the ball hits a defending player's arm or hand in the box, it's either a penalty or it isn't.'

Gary Megson

'You can't get through the game without bookings . . . unless you don't book anyone at all.'

John Hollins

'It's almost impossible for referees these days. They need eyes in the back of their heads, which they haven't got.'

Graham Taylor

'A goal is going to decide this in many ways.'

David O'Leary

'I will always have Arsenal-red blood running through my veins.'

George Graham

'I always say we have a better chance of scoring goals when the ball is in the opposition box.'

Dario Gradi, Crewe Alexandra manager

'When a player gets to 30, so does his body.'

Glenn Hoddle

'If we played like this every week, we wouldn't be so inconsistent.'

Bryan Robson

DRIVING ME CRAZY

Bob Stokoe famously managed Sunderland to a sensational FA Cup final triumph over mighty Leeds in 1973.

According to Ian St John and Jimmy Greaves' book *Funny Old Games*, during a match against Birmingham, Stokoe saw five Sunderland players booked and was less than happy. In fact, he was still fuming when the referee strolled into the dressing-room after the match. The Sunderland team coach was blocking the ref's car, so he asked the manager, 'Is your coach driver here?'

Stokoe replied, 'F*** me, you're not going to book him as well?'

PSYCHOLOGICAL PLOY

The manager of a newly promoted team is concerned that his players don't believe enough in themselves to win the Championship, so he gathers them around in a circle and he says to the one of them, David Smith, 'David, who is the best footballer in England?'

'Umm . . . Cesc Fàbregas?'

'No! You've got to think that *David Smith* is the best footballer in England!'

Thinking that the lads have learned this lesson in sporting psychology, he moves on to the next guy. 'Paul White, who is the best footballer in England?'

'David Smith?'

ABOUT A BALL

The late Alan Ball was one of the many former players who tried his hand at management. An Everton favourite in his playing days, he never managed the team but his popularity at Goodison Park remained undiminished. On one visit, as he was heading into the ground, a fan called over to him, ''Ere, Al pal, gi's yer autograph.'

Ball was carrying bags in both hands and said, 'Can't you see I've got my hands full?'

The fan replied, 'Don't worry, Al pal. Just spit on the paper. That'll do me.'

PRIORITIES

Brian Clough once argued, 'If a chairman sacks the manager he initially appointed, he should go as well.' A manager knows that if his club does badly, his job is on the line; the chairman, on the other hand, can generally afford to be more sanguine. Ipswich chairman John Cobbold was unperturbed when his team were languishing at the foot of the table and the media were saying it was a crisis. Cobbold dismissed the comments, saying, 'The only crisis at this club is when the boardroom runs out of red wine.'

7

BIG RON, BIG MOUTH

'Now Manchester United are 2–1 down on aggregate,
they are in a better position than when they
started the game at 1–1.'

'Big' Ron Atkinson

'There are known knowns. There are things we know that we know. There are known unknowns. That is to say, there are things we now know we don't know. But there are also unknown unknowns. There are things we do not know we don't know.' Thus spoke Donald Rumsfeld, United States Secretary of Defense, in 2002. Like so many of his colleague George W. Bush's remarks ('I know the human being and fish can coexist peacefully'), this baffling comment would seem more appropriate coming from a football pundit, given their unique use of the English language, than from a major-league politician.

Outstanding in this field was Ron Atkinson, until he lost his media work – or, in pundit parlance, took an early bath – in 2004 after he made a racist remark about Chelsea's Marcel Desailly live on TV when he thought his microphone was off during a match in Monaco. Nobody was laughing when Big Ron made that comment.

However, the perpetually tanned and bejewelled 'Mr Bojangles' has devoted his life to entertainment and football, sometimes, it seems, in that order. Generally nobody did it better; baby, despite occasional lapses of taste – in fashion as well as in punditry – Ron was the best. Like David Coleman, Do-Do-Ron-Ron-Ron has given us a new word – 'Ronglish' – because of his spectacularly innovative use of the language of Shakespeare.

BIG RON

Before he began his career as a pundit, Ron was, of course, a manager. In 1981, he succeeded Dave Sexton in the hot seat at Manchester United. A devout Catholic whose reign at the club inspired 'Onward Sexton's Soldiers', an adaptation of the famous hymn, Sexton himself had replaced Tommy Docherty, who, despite having guided United to the FA Cup in 1977, was sacked when it emerged that he had been having an affair with the physio's wife.

It was Sexton who was responsible for Kevin Moran's glittering career at United. Inevitably, given Moran's bravery, throwing his head and body where no sane person would go, injuries came his way. Atkinson once joked that he was going to give Moran a part-time contract because he never finished a match!

Atkinson took the United job having made his name with West Bromwich Albion. In the late 1970s, West Brom were a high-flying team in the old First Division. They went on an end-of-season tour to China, the first English team to visit the country. At one stage, the players were offered the opportunity to visit the Great Wall. One player, when asked his opinion on this wonder of the world, conceded, 'Impressive isn't it?' before adding, 'But once you've seen one wall, you've seen them all.'

THE END IS NIGH

In his book *United to Win*, Atkinson gives an insight into how personality clashes between a player and a manager can end a player's career at a club. When Atkinson succeeded former Leeds stalwart John Giles as manager of West Brom, one of the players he inherited was Irish international Paddy

Mulligan, who had given great service to the club but who was then in the autumn of his career. Ironically enough, Big Ron took an instant dislike to the Irishman in part because of his verbosity, and Mulligan found himself in the reserves.

Atkinson's assistant, Colin Addison, suggested the manager should have a meeting with Mulligan in an effort to lift his spirits. When Paddy arrived in the office, he took the initiative and said, 'Boss, I don't think you like me.'

True to form, Atkinson did not mince his words and replied, 'Paddy, I can't stand you!'

'Can I take it, then, that I'll be going at the end of the season?'

'You can bet money on it!'

After Mulligan left the office, Addison commented, 'Thanks, Ron. I only brought him in so that you could give him a bit of a confidence booster.'

Similarly, when he arrived at Manchester United as manager, Ron was having a chat with a player who realised he was nearing the end of his time at the club. The end was coming faster than he appreciated, though.

'I'm confused,' he said. 'I don't know whether I'm coming or going.'

'My friend,' Atkinson replied, 'I can help you there. You're going.'

MIGHTY MOUTH

After his managerial career went into abeyance, Big Ron took refuge in punditry and immediately made his mark with comments like, 'They only thought the shirts had to go out to get a win.'

As the following selection indicates, Atkinson had no peers for a breathtaking ability to transform mere words and give them new meanings, and his classics will endure forever whenever the history of punditry is written.

'I never comment on referees and I'm not going to break the habit of a lifetime for that prat.'

'The action replay showed it to be worse than it actually was.'

'If Glenn Hoddle said one word to his team at half-time, it was concentration and focus.'

'Liverpool are outnumbered numerically in midfield.'

'I know where he [the referee] should have put his flag up, and he'd have got plenty of help.'

Following a loss at Stamford Bridge, when managing Coventry

'Well, either side could win it, or it could be a draw.'

'Giving the ball away doesn't seem to work in international football.'

'If you score against the Italians, you deserve a goal.'

'I met Mick Jagger when I was playing for Oxford United and the Rolling Stones played a concert there. Little did I know that one day he'd be almost as famous as me.'

'Sometimes you just can't do nothing about anything.'

'They must go for it now, as they have nothing to lose but the match.'

'He dribbles a lot and the opposition don't like it. You can see it all over their faces.'

'Giggs is running long up the backside.'

'I wouldn't say Ginola is the best left-winger in the Premiership, but there are none better.'

'Zidane is not very happy, because he's suffering from the wind.'

'The lad throws it further than I go on holiday.'

'The keeper was unsighted – he still didn't see it.'

CLIVE TYLDESLEY [at the World Cup, as the camera zooms in on a stunning female percussionist in a Brazil shirt]: 'Ron, I didn't know your wife was Brazilian.'
RON ATKINSON: 'I didn't know she played the drums.'

'You can see the ball go past them, or the man, but you'll never see both man and ball go past at the same time. So if the ball goes past, the man won't or if the man goes past they'll take the ball.'

'He's not only a good player, but he's spiteful in the nicest sense of the word.'

'He could have done a lot better there, but full marks to the lad.'

'Yes, Woodcock would have scored, but his shot was just too perfect.'

THE NAKED CHEF

Big Ron has never been known for his tact, and this has given rise to a number of jokes over the years. One story went that Ron was asked to work on a campaign to raise awareness of the dangers of obesity in schools. He decided to call it 'No Child Left with a Big Behind'.

Another had it that on one occasion Big Ron's wife didn't speak to him for three days. It started when she thought she heard a noise downstairs in the middle of the night.

She nudged him and whispered, 'Wake up, wake up!'

'What's the matter?' he asked.

'There are burglars in the kitchen. I think they're eating the beef casserole I made tonight.'

'That'll teach them.'

8

PLAY ON

'The terrible thing about my job is that players get 80 per cent of my earnings.'

Eric Hall, football agent

Clubs do not invest small, and often large, fortunes on players for the sharpness of their intellect or their verbal dexterity. It is probably just as well, as this chapter illustrates. Sometimes, it seems that they are not really tuned in to their environment. Think of Chelsea's Wayne Bridge after the 2007 Carling Cup final win over Arsenal: 'It doesn't matter what happened in the game – we got the three points.' Other times, they are the masters of the obvious. Consider Dave Beasant's comment, 'If you make the right decision, it's normally going to be the correct one.'

SHEAR PLEASURE

Unlike many football stars, Alan Shearer was not a bad boy or a womaniser. In fact, two directors of Newcastle were quoted in an undercover exposé in the *News of the World* calling their star player 'Mary Poppins' and 'boring'. His teammates bought Shearer the video of the musical.

Shearer had sometimes displayed an unusual approach to self-assessment, famously saying, 'One accusation you can't throw at me is that I've always done my best.'

HANGING ON THE TELEPHONE

After Rio Ferdinand missed a drug test, claiming that he'd forgotten about it, the FA did eventually hand down a lengthy ban, although by the time they charged him 86 days had elapsed since the missed test. The punishment would mean the England international would miss the European Championships. It was said that Vodafone were bringing out a new Rio Ferdinand model: it had hardly any memory and took three months to charge.

Ferdinand has often been given a hard time by the press over the years, so perhaps he should remember Brendan Behan's dictum, 'All publicity is good, except an obituary notice.'

MARSH MELLOW

One of the most skilful strikers in English football in the early 1970s was Rodney Marsh. As England struggled to qualify for the 1974 World Cup, their manager Sir Alf Ramsey was feeling under pressure. In their last two matches, England had missed penalties, and Ramsey was seeking volunteers to take penalties before the next match. Everybody declined his invitation. His face lit up when he turned to Marsh. 'Ah, Rodney, surely you'd have the confidence to score a penalty tonight?'

'No problem, boss. It wouldn't cost me a thought. There's just a tiny problem, boss.'

'Oh, what's that?'

'You haven't picked me on the team.'

Another cheeky remark to the dour Ramsey would have serious consequences for his international career. During the team talk before a match, the manager told Marsh that if he didn't work hard enough in the first half he'd be 'pulled off' at half-time, to which Marsh responded, 'Christ! All we get at Manchester City is a cup of tea and an orange!' He never played for England again.

Ramsey wasn't the only manager Marsh wound up. Back when he played for QPR, Rodney greeted their new manager Gordon Jago with: 'Good luck, boss. We're all behind you 50 per cent.'

Rodney was famous for his flair on the pitch and after his retirement found a new career as a pundit with Sky Sports. He always had serious problems with the long-ball game and once observed, 'Wimbledon are putting balls into the blender.'

ODDS ON

Another QPR legend was the England striker Stan Bowles, who was renowned as much for his gambling as for his mercurial talent. One Grand National day, Stan had backed Red Rum. On the pitch during a home match, he heard the race commentary coming from a transistor radio in the crowd as he was back defending a corner. He deliberately kept conceding corners for the next few minutes so that he could continue to listen to the commentary. As soon as he heard that his horse had come in, he cleared the ball up the field and went on to play the game of his life.

Ernie Tagg, his manager at Crewe Alexandra, said of Bowles' gambling compulsion: 'If Stan could pass a betting shop like he can pass a ball, he'd have no worries at all.'

In 1976, Liverpool 'stole' the league title from QPR in the last match of the season with a victory over Wolves. That may explain Bowles' comment, 'Liverpool are my nap selection. I prefer to sleep when they're on the box.'

POKER FACE

Stan Bowles is asked what he does after he's lost a lot of money at the races.

'I go home and play cards with my dog,' he answers.

'Good gracious, you must have a very clever dog.'

'Not really. Every time he gets a good hand, he wags his tail.'

EVERYONE'S A CRITIC

It may be a privileged life being a football player today, but you do have to put up with a fair bit of criticism. Take this crushing verdict on Didi Hamann's performance by a BBC Radio Manchester commentator: 'There is very little movement from Manchester City's midfield players. In fact, if they are planning on playing Dietmar Hamann in their next game they will have to write to the council for permission.' Or how about this Olympic-level piece of sarcasm from Jimmy Greaves: 'Stevie G, we hail thee. Few can play so many dummies. Shaping to pass to a teammate and then completely outwitting him by giving it to the opposition.'

There's no guarantee that your manager will be complimentary about you, either – not even when he's trying. Here's Harry Redknapp on Kanu's aerial threat: 'Kanu has been fantastic. My God, we've even got him heading the ball. Well, it's not really heading, more like hitting him on the head.'

WALK TALL

The last time QPR were in the Premiership they were managed by Ray Wilkins. After they were relegated to Division One, they came up against Oxford United, featuring Kevin Francis, who is 6 ft 7 in. tall, giving a whole new meaning to 'the big league'. Afterwards, Wilkins gave his opinion of Francis: 'To be fair, he's got quite a good touch, but he's quite daunting. If I ever need my guttering fixed, I'll give him a call.'

TEAM SPIRIT

Former Arsenal goalkeeper Jens Lehmann had a reputation for being a bit, let's say . . . different. During his last season at Borussia Dortmund, he sprinted after another player and grabbed him around the neck, earning a red card. Nothing unusual about that, you might say, but the other player was Marcio Amoroso – one of his own defenders.

Fulham legend Johnny Haynes knew what it was like to experience a lack of team spirit, once stating, 'Sometimes at Fulham you feel as if you're not so much passing the ball as passing the buck.'

PASSED ON

Many years ago at a press conference, one daft footballer, whose name has been lost in the mists of time, noticed that a long-serving journalist was not in attendance and asked where he was.

'He died very suddenly,' another hack told him.

'How did he die?'

'It was the big C.'

'Could he not swim?'

ALL IN THE GAME

Unusual post-goal celebrations have long been a feature of soccer matches, but their ever-increasing oddness is a constant source of amusement. The birthplace of the bizarre is the samba-land that is Brazil. Many players are known for celebrating their goals enthusiastically, but the award for the most surreal celebration must go to an Atlético Mineiro striker for his performance after scoring in the Belo Horizonte derby against América, who rejoice in the nickname 'the Rabbits'. The humorous hitman raced to the home fans, removed a carrot from his shorts and proceeded to eat it in what was described as 'a mocking manner'. A World Cup referee in the TV commentary box observed that the player should have been booked, but then admitted that eating a carrot that had spent 20 minutes down his shorts was a punishment to fit the crime.

Another example of the 'it's not how you score, it's the way that you show it' motif comes from a 1998 Flamengo v. Fluminense game, the so-called 'Fla–Flu' derby, at the Maracaña Stadium in Rio. This hallowed stadium is famous for holding the world attendance record – 199,854 people squeezed in for the 1950 Brazil v. Uruguay World Cup match – but it is also interesting for a payphone installed behind one of the goals in front of the terracing. One clever scorer made a beeline for the phone and proceeded to make a call, no doubt to his agent to request that he add another nought to his transfer price. Where he kept his coins remains open to speculation, although he may have been friends with the carrot man. The celebration has now caught on, although rumours that a phone company are to provide each player with a mobile phone to prevent queuing in high-scoring games are as yet unconfirmed.

NOT WORTH THE PAPER IT'S WRITTEN ON

Former Chelsea star John Hollins must have got some bemused looks when he remarked, 'A contract on a piece of paper saying you want to leave is like a piece of paper saying you want to leave.'

PSYCHO

Few players commanded more respect than Nottingham Forest's Stuart Pearce, whose nickname was 'Psycho'. In his case, Forest fans believed it was not the winning but the taking someone apart that counted. In 1992, Pearce left everyone scratching their heads in bemusement and amusement with his unforgettable observation, 'I can see the carrot at the end of the tunnel.'

Pearce's image as the punk-loving hard man of English football took a bit of a knock when he was managing Manchester City. Before a match against West Ham following a run of poor results, his daughter insisted that her stuffed toy horse Beanie sit with him on the touchline. 'It's difficult explaining to a seven year old that this is the Premiership and I'm known as Psycho,' said Pearce. But City won 2–0, and Beanie returned for several matches. He was credited with a winning streak and became a crowd favourite but lost his place after a bad defeat to Wigan. 'It has been retired,' commented Pearce. 'It was gelded after last week. I had to knock its rocks off. It was not so much a lucky mascot any more. But my daughter, Chelsea, is glad to have him back.'

GUN CONTROL

Some players do not react well to being dropped. In 1990, Howard Wilkinson had been picking Vinnie Jones for Leeds United's first team less and less often. One day, on the coach to an away game, Vinnie, who was a keen shot and was off to a shoot later that weekend, appeared beside Wilkinson at the front of the coach with his double-barrelled shotgun in his hand. Jokingly pointing the gun at the shocked manager, he asked, 'Well, boss, am I playing this weekend?'

You can see why Wimbledon gaffer Joe Kinnear once answered the question 'What is the most outrageous thing you have ever bought?' with the words 'Vinnie Jones'.

At one stage, Vinnie's main claim to fame was an infamous photograph of him grabbing the private parts of the young Paul Gascoigne in a match between Wimbledon and Newcastle, momentarily making Gazza an honorary member of the Bee Gees. As a result, when playing against Vinnie those opposition strikers who were less than enthusiastic about the physical side of the game tended to spend so much time with their hands over their private parts that they ought to have been renamed Holden McGroin.

Jones might be said to have a rather strange sense of humour. Tony Cascarino has recalled that in 1994 Vinnie volunteered to organise Chelsea's Christmas party. His idea of a good time was a dwarf-throwing contest. Two dwarfs were hired, with appropriate protective gear, and thrown around a pub with wanton abandon.

Hollywood, surprisingly perhaps, came knocking on Vinnie's door and made him into a movie star. The football-watching public has lost out on a unique voice as a pundit. On the other hand, Vinnie's track record makes you wonder whether this might be a blessing in disguise, given comments like, 'Winning doesn't really matter as long as you win.'

IT'S ONLY WORDS

Players have given football-speak a popular currency, especially through their post-retirement gigs as commentators. However, they often make fans cringe when they open their mouths, as this baker's dozen shows:

1. 'Football's football; if that weren't the case, it wouldn't be the game it is.'

   Garth Crooks

2. 'The only thing that Norwich didn't get was the goal that they finally got.'

   Jimmy Greaves

3. IAN ST JOHN: 'Is he speaking to you yet?'

   JIMMY GREAVES: 'Not yet, but I hope to be incommunicado with him in a very short space of time.'

4. 'Tempo – now there's a big word.'

   Barry Venison

5. 'Yes, he is not unused to playing in midfield, but at the same time he's not used to playing there either.'

   Emlyn Hughes

6. 'I've always been a childhood Liverpool fan, even when I was a kid.'

   Harry Kewell

7. COMMENTATOR: 'Has Emile Heskey something to prove against his former club?'

   DAVID PLATT: 'No, not at all. But he will want to show they were wrong to sell him.'

8. 'I sent around a text message saying, "This is Gary Neville's new mobile number." A few minutes later, my

phone beeped with a reply saying, "So what?" That was Roy's sense of humour.'

Gary Neville finds out how much Keano's been missing him

9. 'Paolo Di Canio is capable of scoring the goal he scored.'

Bryan Robson

10. 'I am not dreaming about Arsenal. You need huge qualities to go there and there are already so many great players at the club. If I have the chance to go to England, I will aim on a level below Arsenal. I like Tottenham very much.'

Lens midfielder Antoine Sibierski

11. 'Everything in our favour was against us.'

Danny Blanchflower

12. 'Arsenal are streets ahead of everyone in this league and Manchester United are up there with them, obviously.'

Craig Bellamy in 2003

13. 'He hit the post, and after the game people will say, "Well, he hit the post."'

Jimmy Greaves

DOCTOR, DOCTOR

Football is a tough game and it, along with the lifestyle, can really take its toll on players in later life.

One retired player went to the hospital and said, 'I get terrible headaches, blackouts and dizzy spells, and I find it hard to concentrate.'

The doctor enquired, 'What age are you, sir?'

'Only 30.'

The doctor raised his eyebrows. 'So your memory's affected too?'

Another was talking to his doctor before an operation. 'Are you sure,' he asked, 'that I'll recover? I've heard that doctors sometimes give wrong diagnoses, treat patients for kidney problems and they later die of something else.'

'That's nonsense,' said the doctor. 'If I treat a patient for kidney problems, he dies of kidney problems.'

HIGH SPIRITS

When England international Terry Fenwick was charged with a drink-driving offence, his close friend Terry Venables observed, making an unfortunate choice of words, 'The spirit he has shown is second to none.'

HAIR-RAISING

One of the stars of England's 1966 World Cup-winning team was Bobby Charlton. Even in his playing days, Bobby was follically challenged. He tried to disguise his hair loss with a combover.

Bobby wasn't always on the best of terms with George Best, so it's no surprise that Best poked fun at Bobby's lack of hair, telling spoof chat-show hostess Mrs Merton, 'I sent my son to one of his schools of excellence and he came back bald.'

HELPFUL ADVICE

One day, when his hair-loss troubles are just beginning, Bobby Charlton goes to the club doctor to ask for help.

'My hair's starting to fall out,' he says. 'Can you think of anything I can use to keep it in?'

'How about a cardboard box?'

GONE BUT NOT FORGOTTEN

Bobby's wife is out with a group of friends for a meal. One notices that Mrs Charlton is wearing a lovely locket and says,

'It's beautiful. I suppose you carry a memento of some sort in it?'

Mrs Charlton replies, 'Yes, it's a lock of Bobby's hair.'

'But Bobby's alive and well.'

'I know, but his hair's long gone.'

BIG JACK

Bobby's brother Jack, like so many former players, has had a go at football punditry. He has produced the odd memorable moment in that role, such as: 'It was a fair decision, the penalty, even though it was debatable whether it was inside or outside the box,' and 'It was a definite penalty, but Wright made a right swansong of it.'

BY NAME AND BY NATURE

Robbie Savage is considered one of a dying breed of old-school, tough-tackling defenders, giving rise to a riddle.

Q: Why does Robbie Savage make football a colourful game?

A: Everyone ends up black and blue.

THE WRITE STUFF

Graeme Le Saux – along with Pat Nevin, one of the game's few intellectuals – having retired from football, professes a desire to become a great writer. An interviewer asks him to define 'great' and he says, 'I want to write stuff that the whole world will read, stuff that people will react to on a truly emotional level, stuff that will make them scream, cry, howl in pain and anger.' The next day, he's offered a job writing error messages for Microsoft.

LAST MAN STANDING

So bad was the fog during a match played in the Second World War that Charlton goalkeeper Sam Bartram was tapped on the shoulder by a policeman who told him that the game had been abandoned and he was the only player left on the field.

A MIXED BAG

Sometimes it seems that footballers have provided as much entertainment simply by opening their mouths and speaking as they have by dazzling on the pitch. The following collection provides the evidence.

'The referee was booking everyone. I thought he was filling in his lottery numbers.'

Ian Wright

'I don't really believe in targets, because my next target is to beat Stoke City.'

Ron Wylie

'Yeah, I was a bit anxious when I got to the stadium, but, in all fairness, if I hadn't been anxious, I'd have been worried.'

Paul Robinson

'Leeds is a great club and it's been my home for years, even though I live in Middlesbrough.'

Jonathan Woodgate

'I wouldn't be bothered if we lost every game as long as we won the league.'

Mark Viduka

'Football is a game of skill. We kicked them a bit and they kicked us a bit.'

Graham Roberts

'I'm as happy as I can be, but I have been happier.'

Ugo Ehiogu

RICHARD KEYS: 'Well, wasn't that the most nail-biting and dramatic finale?'

ALAN SHEARER: 'Yeah, especially at the end.'

'There's never a good time to score an own goal against yourself.'

John Greig

'I can't promise anything but I can promise 100 per cent.'

Paul Power

'The game is finely balanced with Celtic well on top.'

John Greig

'I always used to put my right boot on first, and then obviously my right sock.'

Barry Venison

'The FA Cup final is a great occasion, but only until ten minutes before the kick-off. Then the players come on and we ruin the whole thing.'

Danny Blanchflower

'It was a Boxing Day boxing match.'

Patrick Vieira on a melee during a Chelsea–Arsenal match on 26 December

'That was extremely disappointing and there can't be any excuses. Chances seemed to go into the goalkeeper's hands, freak goals went against us and the referee was petty.'

Gary Neville

'I've had to give Stanley a telling-off. He was crossing the ball with the lace facing me.'

Tommy Lawton pays tribute to the
accuracy of Stanley Matthews

'Joe has got broad shoulders and big nuts.'

John Terry on Joe Cole

'There's only one club in Europe that you can leave Manchester United for – Real Madrid or Barcelona.'

John Aldridge

'When Charlie Cooke sold you a dummy, you had to pay to get back into the ground.'

Jim Baxter

'We didn't come here for a draw, or any other result.'

John Terry

'The only thing I have in common with George Best is that we came from the same place, play for the same club and were discovered by the same man.'

Norman Whiteside

INTERVIEWER: 'You've devoted a whole chapter of your book to Jimmy Greaves.'

PAT JENNINGS: 'That's right. Well, what can you say about Jimmy Greaves?'

TAKING IT EASY

When he was Liverpool goalkeeper, David James paid tribute to his illustrious predecessor Bruce Grobbelaar, saying, 'I remember one game when Liverpool were 6–0 up, and someone handed him an umbrella and he just sat there by the post, out of the rain.'

THE DEMON DRINK

In the early '90s, Everton went on a pre-season tour to Spain. Peter Beagrie's celebrations after a match with Real Sociedad were a little over-enthusiastic and of the liquid variety. Beagrie got a lift back to the hotel on the back of a motorbike, courtesy of a friendly local. When he failed to get the attention of the night porter and gain entry to the hotel, Beagrie got up on the bike and drove through a plate-glass window. The problem, apart from anything else, was that he'd got the wrong hotel.

GOOD SELECTION?

To show that misfortune afflicts players for both Merseyside teams, former Liverpool striker Robbie Keane got into a bit of a muddle when he said, 'The penalty – I have to choose my words very carefully – it was a disgrace.'

LEGS ELEVEN

Keane's predecessor at Anfield, Peter Crouch, is known for his unusual physique. Hence Chris Waddle's memorable description: 'Peter Crouch is starting to look a bit leggy up front.' When Crouch moved to Portsmouth, a fan remarked, 'He's so thin he needs to run around the shower to get wet.' Chants directed at him have included 'Freak!' and 'You should have been an X-Man!' Arsène Wenger described him as 'a basketball player' and David O'Leary called him 'a lovely big bag of bones'.

The fans at Liverpool loved him, though, especially after he unveiled his robotic-dance goal celebration. Said Steven Gerrard, 'The fans have taken to Crouchy. We're not sure if that's because of his play or the dance. At least his dancing is better than his penalty taking!'

WELSH WIZARDS

In the 1980s, Wales had two of the greatest strikers in the game: Ian Rush and Mark Hughes. A print journalist was reading his column down the line to the paper's office. He said: 'There are those who would say Rush and Hughes are the most dangerous strikers in Europe.' He was shocked to read the next morning: 'There are those who would say Russian Jews are the most dangerous strikers in Europe.'

THE BATTLE OF THE BULGE

A distinguished goalkeeper was coming towards the end of his playing days, as was evident from his receding hairline and rapidly expanding waistline. When he missed a cross that allowed the opposition to score a soft goal, a fan shouted at him, 'I bet you would have caught it if it was a beefburger!'

FAMOUS QUOTE

Geoff Hurst prompted the most famous quote in football when he scored the winning goal in the 1966 World Cup final: 'They think it's all over. It is now.' When Hurst appeared on *The Weakest Link* and was asked by Anne Robinson, 'Which "K" is Britain's most widespread bird of prey?' he replied, 'Eagle.'

A VERBAL LEGACY

Every year, the Professional Footballers' Association honours its members for their achievements on the pitch. As the following selection illustrates, it may be time for them to start handing out the gongs for making and inspiring funny remarks, too.

'The performance today shows that other teams are going to have to score more goals than us if they want to beat us.'

Darren Bent

'In the cold light of day, you go to bed at night thinking about the chances you've missed.'

David Platt

'Look at the way people look up to Jodie Marsh and Jordan. But what are they actually famous for? Well, apart from the obvious.'

David Bentley keeps
abreast of the big questions

'Poor Scott Carson. Just two more hands and another chest and he could have saved it.'

Jimmy Greaves after Carson's goalkeeping
howler against Croatia in 2007

'Do I stay in touch with Phil? I wasn't that friendly with him. I went to his wedding. That was enough.'

Roy Keane on the depth of his relationship with Phil Neville

'Man United's defensive record is second to none. Apart from Liverpool's that is.'

Warren Barton

'Of course, Steven Gerrard is one of only a few Liverpool players who never get left out by Rafa. And even he doesn't always get picked.'

David Pleat

'Without doubt, there is more quality in Spain. If I am watching a West Ham–Bolton game, it almost sends me to sleep.'

Cesc Fàbregas

'Your legs are gone. You're too old. You're too slow.'

Cheery text message reportedly sent from Craig Bellamy's phone
to Alan Shearer after Newcastle lost in a 2005 FA Cup semi-final

'There's only one person who knows how he missed that and that's Wayne Rooney, and even he doesn't know.'

George Graham

'He is playing better than ever, even if he is going grey and looking like a pigeon.'

Gianluca Vialli on Mark Hughes

'Any manager will tell you they'd rather win one and lose two than draw three, because you get more points.'

Les Ferdinand

'Paul Scholes with four players in front of him – five if you count Gary Neville.'

RTÉ's Darragh Maloney

'The 2,000 away fans will be unhappy. In fact, half of them have gone: there's only 500 left.'

Chris Waddle

'A lot of people phoned to wish me a speedy recovery and I thank them all. I have spoken to Cantona, Thuram, Henry, Vieira. Even some people who I don't know and who I have not heard of before, people like Dion Dublin.'

Liverpool's Djibril Cissé, after breaking his leg

'I will never say a bad word against Gérard Houllier, but if he had stayed I would have wanted to leave.'

Milan Baros

'Joe Cole had a slash on the edge of the box and it actually found its way back to the corner flag.'

BBC Radio 5 Live's Colin Cooper

'Bobby Gould thinks I'm trying to stab him in the back. In fact, I'm right behind him.'

Stuart Pearson

'John Terry's an extra-terrestrial – I think he's from Mars. He's like E.T., he needs to phone home.'

Claudio Ranieri

'Shearer could be at 100 per cent fitness, but not peak fitness.'

Graham Taylor

MANISH BHASIN: 'There's a story that Ruud van Nistelrooy may sign for Spurs.'

GAVIN PEACOCK: 'No. He's a top striker.'

'The first time I met Wayne [Rooney] was at an awards ceremony. Everyone was talking about him being a really good player but not able to communicate. So I said to Wayne, "You probably find speaking a little bit difficult, but the more you do it the better you'll get."'

Bobby Charlton encourages and insults simultaneously

'I find football an easy game. It's the other players on the pitch who make it hard.'

Len Shackleton

KEEP YOUR HAIR ON

England hero Bobby Moore, who captained his country to the World Cup in 1966, was playing for West Ham against Newcastle one day at St James' Park. He went to the centre circle for the coin toss and noticed that the referee, Ricky Nicholson, had a great head of hair. As the match progressed, Moore was shocked to see that the ref had become completely bald. The official explained, 'It's in my pocket. I washed it last night and I don't want it blowing off and getting dirty.'

NOBBY

Nobby Stiles was one of Moore's teammates on England's World Cup-winning side. Stiles' brother-in-law is Leeds legend John Giles. In Giles' final season with Manchester United, both he and Stiles were in and out of the side. According to George Best's *The Best of Times*, Matt Busby had a habit of asking Nobby how he was playing. Invariably, Stiles would say, 'OK,' and then Busby would inform him he was dropped. Giles advised his friend that he was handling the manager all wrong. When he was asked how he was playing, he should always say he was playing brilliantly and that the team couldn't do without him. Stiles took this advice the next time the manager questioned him in that way. The only problem was that Busby asked an unexpected supplementary question: 'Yes, but can you play better?'

'Yes,' was Nobby's instinctive reply.

'You're dropped for the next match,' was the boss's riposte.

EYESORE

Playing for Man United against Burnley under floodlights at Old Trafford, Stiles badly mistimed a tackle on Andy Lochhead. The referee, Pat Partridge, went to book him. Nobby pleaded, 'But it's the floodlights, ref. They shine in my contact lenses and I can't see a bloody thing.' The unmoved ref started to write Nobby's name in the book and misspelled his name, writing 'Styles'.

'Ah, ref, you can't even get my name right,' Nobby complained.

The ref responded, 'I'm surprised you can read with the floodlights shining on your contact lenses.'

Nobby had to laugh: 'Nice one. Spell it any way you like.'

THE CLOWN PRINCE

Len Shackleton was known for his skill on the field and his humour off it, hence his nickname, 'the Clown Prince of Soccer'. He had tremendous control and was able to perform tricks that made him a hero for the crowds. He gained a reputation for outrageous showmanship, one example being the time at Highbury when he dribbled the ball down the field and into Arsenal's penalty area, where he stopped, standing with one foot on the ball, and mimed combing his hair and looking at his watch.

In 1948, he signed to Sunderland from Newcastle for a then-record fee of £20,500. 'Shack', as he was also known, was adored by Sunderland fans for his goals. He scored 101 for the club and grew so loyal to them that he once said of rivals Newcastle, 'I'm not biased when it comes to Newcastle – I don't care who beats them.'

His five England caps were considered a paltry return for his class, but when one selector was asked to explain why Shackleton was so often omitted from the team, he replied, 'Because we play at Wembley stadium, not the London Palladium.' Shackleton later commented, 'I suppose I should have been flattered.'

During one match for Sunderland, Shackleton was unhappy with the referee's stewardship of the game and kept complaining to him. In frustration, the ref, Arthur Ellis, later to find fame on *It's a Knockout*, asked, 'Who's refereeing this match – me or you?'

Len replied: 'To tell you the truth, neither of us.'

9

CARRY ON COMMENTATING

———●———

*'I've always said there's a place for the press
but they haven't dug it yet.'*

Tommy Docherty

The role of the media is variously to inform, educate, enlighten and entertain. Sometimes the football journalists manage all four at once, notably in the *Sunday Times* headline announcing the replay date after Arsenal and Sheffield Wednesday drew in the 1993 FA Cup final: 'Arsenal, Wednesday, Thursday'. Often the headlines are at their most entertaining when they are putting the boot in, as in *The Sun*'s malicious verdict on the Intertoto Cup: 'The InterTwoBob Cup'. The media's cruelty isn't always deliberate. The following sentence, which appeared in a computer magazine, seems a bit unfair on Chelsea, even in 1988: 'Commodore already sponsors Tessa Sanderson, Chelsea FC and a football team, Bayern Munich.'

While the media may aim for enlightenment, they sometimes create confusion.

John Inverdale: 'What do you think the score will be?'

Caller to 5 Live: 'Nil–all draw.'

Inverdale: 'So who'll score for Everton then?'

In the light of such incisive analysis, it is perhaps not surprising that Roy Keane is so dismissive of football pundits, having said, 'I wouldn't listen to these people in the pub and yet they're on television constantly,' and, 'I wouldn't trust some of these people to walk my dog.'

Nonetheless, for their services to the entertainment industry this chapter pays homage to football's fourth estate, beginning with a living legend.

MOTTY

Who else could have come up with 'The goals made such a difference to the way this game went' but the BBC icon John Motson OBE, football's best-known Barnet supporter, who sprang to national prominence when reporting Hereford's shock 2–1 FA Cup replay win against Newcastle United in 1972. One of his more recent memorable comments came in the 2008 FA Cup final when, incredulous, he said, 'Portsmouth think they've scored,' only for his co-commentator Mark Lawrenson to interject, 'That's because they have, John.'

In 2001, a speech therapist found that for rhythm, pitch, volume and tone, Motson scored the highest among Britain's top sports commentators. He is a national institution because of his sheepskin coat, penchant for statistics and comments like those below, a football team of Motty moments.

1. 'It's Arsenal 0, Everton 1, and the longer it stays like that, the more you've got to fancy Everton to win.'

2. 'Koller shares a hairstyle with Jaap Stam. Of course, they have no hair.'

3. 'The match has become quite unpredictable, but it still looks as though Arsenal will win the cup.'

4. 'Nearly all the Brazilian supporters are wearing yellow shirts. It's a fabulous kaleidoscope of colour!'

5. MOTTY: 'Well, Trevor, what does this substitution mean tactically?'

    TREVOR BROOKING: 'Well, Barnes has come off and Rocastle has come on . . .'

6. 'Not the first half you might have expected, even though the score might suggest that it was.'

7. 'There's been a colour clash. Both teams are wearing white.'

8. 'For those of you watching in black and white, Spurs are playing in yellow.'

9. MOTTY: 'Say something, Mark.'
   [Pause.]
   LAWRO: 'I can't.'

10. 'Northern Ireland were in white, which was quite appropriate because three inches of snow had to be cleared from the pitch before kick-off.'

11. 'The Argentinians are numbered alphabetically.'

   Subs' Bench
   'Reinders is standing on the ball with Breitner, and Muller has gone to join them.'

   'There is still nothing on the proverbial scoreboard.'

ONE FOR THE FACT FANS

Incredibly, Motty's diligent research does not always get the respect it deserves. Witness the following exchange:

MOTTY: 'Bramall Lane is a fantastic place, and I believe one of the only grounds to host an FA Cup final and Test match cricket.'

LAWRO: 'Stay in last night, did you, John?'

THE POST-MORTEM

Despite their valiant efforts, interviewers don't always manage to get the best out of players.

JOURNALIST: 'What did you do after the Romanian defeat?'

DAVID SEAMAN: 'We talked over everything, the things that went right and the things that didn't work out. Then we studied the videos very carefully.'

JOURNALIST: 'Why do you think you lost, then?'

SEAMAN: 'Well, it were just one of those things.'

THE STAR OF DAVID

England goalkeeper David James was interviewed by *FHM* magazine. One line of questioning began as follows:

INTERVIEWER: 'French author Albert Camus, a fellow goalkeeper, once wrote, "One sentence will suffice for the modern man: he fornicated and read the papers." Doesn't that describe modern football? Shagging birds and then reading about it?'

JAMES: 'No.'

INTERVIEWER: 'No? Can't you elaborate a bit? I spent ages on that question.'

JAMES: 'I don't read the papers.'

FACTUALLY CORRECT

A plane was about to crash in an isolated area and one of the passengers was lucky enough to be able to find a parachute and escape. He landed on top of a very tall tree but had no idea where he was and was unable to move. After a while, Alan Hansen walked by. The parachutist shouted down, 'Excuse me, sir, do you know where I am?'

Hansen calmly replied, 'You're on top of a tree.'

The survivor had a second question. 'By any chance, are you a football pundit?'

Hansen was astounded. 'Yes I am. How could you guess?'

'It was very simple, really. The information you gave me was correct but absolutely useless.'

PUBLIC SERVICE BROADCASTING

Steve Rider slightly missed the point with this helpful piece of advice for viewers: 'The match will be shown on *Match of the Day* this evening. If you don't want to know the result, look away now as we show you Tony Adams lifting the trophy for Arsenal.'

THE NUMBERS GAME

Over the years, football commentators have often got themselves into trouble with numbers. In the circumstances, a baker's dozen of mathematical mishaps seems the most appropriate.

1. 'Aston Villa are seventh in the league – that's almost as high as you can get without being one of the top six.'

    Ian Payne

2. 'Brentford reserves were involved in a nine-goal thriller when they beat Orient 4–3.'

    Ealing Gazette

3. 'That could have been his second yellow card . . . if he'd already got his first one, of course.'

    Trevor Brooking

4. 'And Ritchie has now scored 11 goals, exactly double the number he scored last season.'

    Alan Parry

5. 'Never go for a 50–50 ball unless you are 80–20 sure of winning it.'

Ian Drake

6. 'It's a game of two teams.'

Peter Brackley

7. 'I don't know if that result's enough to lift Birmingham off the bottom of the table, although it'll certainly take them above Sunderland.'

Mike Ingham

8. 'Plenty of goals in Divisions Three and Four today. Darlington nil, Hereford nil.'

Announcer on BBC Radio 2

9. 'Ian Rush, deadly ten times out of ten, but that wasn't one of them.'

Peter Jones

10. 'Spurs, one of the in-form teams of the moment with successive wins, are almost as impressive as Queens Park Rangers with five.'

Bob Wilson

11. 'He has all-round, 365-degree vision.'

Alan Mullery

12. 'You wouldn't be surprised if England went on and won 9–0.'

*Alan Hansen discussing a match in which
the score was already 2–2*

13. 'So that's 1–0. Sounds like the score at Boundary Park, where of course it's 2–2.'

Jack Wainwright

THE DARK SIDE

Q: How many pundits does it take to change a light bulb?
A: None. They just sit there in the dark and complain.

DOCTOR'S ORDERS

Five surgeons are discussing what kind of person makes the best patient for them to operate on. The first surgeon says, 'Accountants are the best because when you open them up, everything inside is numbered.'

The second responds, 'Try electricians. Everything inside them is colour coded.'

The third surgeon says, 'No, I like librarians. Everything inside them is in alphabetical order.'

The fourth surgeon interjects, 'I prefer construction workers. They always understand when it takes longer than you expect and you have a few parts left over at the end.'

To which the fifth surgeon says: 'You're all wrong. Football pundits are the easiest. There's no guts, no brain and their heads are interchangeable with their arses.'

DOG-GONE

The written word is open to interpretation. To illustrate: a little girl is attacked by a vicious Alsatian in Leeds, but she's rescued by a young man in a Leeds United jersey who comes along and saves the day by killing the dog. The local newspaper sends down a journalist to cover the story. He tells the locals that it's a great story and says, 'Tomorrow, we'll run a story headlined: "Leeds United Football Star Saves Girl".' The witnesses patiently explain to him that he can't do that because the young man doesn't actually play for Leeds, he was just wearing a replica top.

The journalist thinks for a moment and says, 'That's OK. We'll put: "Leeds Man Saves Girl from Alsatian".' They explain that he can't do that either because the young man is a recent 'blow-in' and has only lived in the city for a short time.

The following day, the headline that appears in the paper is: 'Evil Monster Kills Family Pet'.

BONFIRE OF THE VANITIES

Many footballers' attitude to the press can be summed up in a story of God and the Devil. On the first day, God created the sun; the Devil countered and created sunburn. On the second day, God created sex; the Devil created marriage. On the third day, God created a journalist. The Devil deliberated throughout the fourth day and on the fifth day he created another journalist.

OUTSIDE THE BOX

Why do journalists get such a bad press from footballers? Consider the time when *Vanity Fair* interviewed Arsenal's Freddie Ljungberg and asked him whether he waxed his bottom and who in the dressing-room had the biggest lunchbox.

PRISON BREAK

A new inmate was learning about life in prison from his cellmate and asked, 'Do you watch much television here?'

'Only Ian Wright's football analysis.'

'That's too bad. Still it's nice that the governor lets you watch that at least.'

'It's not nice,' replies the cellmate. 'It's the toughest part of our punishment.'

A MODERN-DAY MIRACLE

It's a little-known fact, but some football fans think of Ian Wright as a life-saver and a miracle-worker. One Spurs supporter was in a horrific car crash and was on a life-support machine for several weeks. All kinds of prayers were said and holy medals were placed on his forehead, but to no avail. As he was a mad football fan, someone, in a fit of desperation, wheeled a TV in to his bedside and stuck on a video of *Match of the Day* featuring Wright. As soon as Wright had made his first comments, the comatose patient got up from his bed and switched off the TV. As the astonished doctors and nurses looked on, he said, 'That f***ing idiot was wrecking my head.'

CHIN UP

Few facial features have ever been as remarked on by football fans as the chin of Jimmy Hill, for years the presenter of *Match of the Day*. When Jimmy Hill was the chairman of Fulham, his club was due to face an FA inquiry after some of the players had been involved in a brawl after a match with Gillingham. Hill set out to prove that Fulham should not be held responsible with a video presentation showing the game's flashpoints. He was very pleased with his efforts and boasted to friends before the inquiry that the FA should be selling tickets for his presentation. The only problem was that when he produced his video as evidence he was shocked to discover that his wife had taped a cookery programme over it!

READ ON

Jimmy Hill once had the job of closing the *Match of the Day* programme by giving viewers the address to which they could send their nominations for the Goal of the Month competition. He had to give them the address twice and, rather than writing the whole sentence twice, the person who had prepared the cue card had just added the appropriate instruction. Jimmy gave the address as: 'Goal of the Month, BBC Television, Wood Lane, Shepherd's Bush, London W12 – read twice.'

It was also Jimmy who asserted that Romania's success in the 1998 World Cup group matches could be attributed in part to the players having dyed their hair peroxide blond as a team bonding exercise. According to him, it made it easier for them to see their passing options.

TAKE TO THE HILLS

Jimmy Hill has added to the gaiety of the nation with some arresting comments. Hill's magnificent seven gaffes are:

1. 'England now have three fresh men, with three fresh legs.'

2. 'He has two feet, which a lot of players don't have nowadays.'

3. 'Manchester United are looking to Frank Stapleton to pull some magic out of the fire.'

4. 'Despite the rain, it's still raining here at Old Trafford.'

5. 'We're not used to weather in June in this country.'

6. 'It wasn't a bad performance, but you can't tell whether it was good or bad.'

7. 'It's a cup final and the one who wins it goes through.'

THINK BEFORE SPEAKING

There are all kinds of potential pitfalls facing a television pundit. During Harold Macmillan's time as Prime Minister, he received a grave message about a diplomatic disaster during a parliamentary recess. BBC radio reported the event as follows: 'These dismal tidings were delivered to the PM on the golf course, where he was playing a round with Lady Dorothy.' The words read fine in print, but when spoken the sentence took on a very different connotation!

STRAIGHT SHOOTING

Alan Hansen does not mince his words. The gruff Scot calls it as it is. But timing is everything in football punditry, as in life. During the 1994 World Cup in the USA, Hansen commented on the poor positioning of a defender in the Argentina–Nigeria match: 'He wants shooting for a mistake like that.' Just a few days earlier, the Colombian central defender Andrés Escobar – scorer of an own goal in Colombia's 2–1 defeat by the USA – had been shot dead in his home town of Medellín. It was not Hansen's finest hour.

SALT AND LINEKER

Star of the Walkers crisps adverts Gary Lineker, known as 'Big Ears' ever since the sticky-out features were mocked each week on *They Think It's All Over*, was referred to as 'Junior Des' by his England teammates because of his punditry ambitions. In the early days, he struggled as Des's replacement as anchor for the BBC's soccer coverage. His most notable gaffe came in a Montpellier–Manchester United match when he was describing the poor condition of the pitch and said, 'Most of the players will be wearing rubbers tonight.' Another classic was: 'There's no in between – you're either good or bad. We were in between.'

NO LOVE

It's good when pundits have a bit of an edge to their comments. I might not be the biggest fan in the world of the BBC's soccer coverage, but I did enjoy, during the 2002 World Cup, Martin O'Neill's comment to Gary Lineker: 'You know what I like about you, Gary? Very little.'

THE ORIGINAL OF THE SPECIES

Gary Lineker is a mere novice in the howler stakes compared with the peerless David Coleman, whose prodigious talents and crimes against the English language are such that *Private Eye* coined a new word to describe commentator gaffes: 'Colemanballs'.

Coleman's name is linked with drama, particularly in athletics, and he is known for an excitable style that led Clive

James to comment, 'Anything that matters so much to David Coleman, you realise, doesn't matter so much at all.'

The following are my favourite Coleman blunders.

'That's the fastest time ever run, but it's not as fast as the world record.'

'The late start is due to the time.'

'Her time was 4 minutes 13 seconds, which she is capable of.'

'This could be a repeat of what will happen at the European Games next week.'

'This race is all about racing.'

'David Bedford is the athlete of all time in the 1970s.'

'It doesn't mean anything, but what it does mean is that Abdi Bile is very relaxed.'

'There is Brendan Foster, by himself, with 20,000 people.'

'And with an alphabetical irony Nigeria follows New Zealand.'

'She's not Ben Johnson, but then who is?'

'I hope the Romanian doesn't get through, because I can't pronounce her bloody name.'

'Lasse Virén, the champion, came in fifth and ran a champion's race.'

'His brother failed, so let's see if he can succeed and maintain the family tradition.'

'They came through absolutely together, with Alan Wells in first place.'

'The reason she's so fast over hurdles is because she's so fast between them.'

'Panetta was the silver medallist in the European Championships, when he led all the way.'

'The big guns haven't pulled all the stops out.'

'The news from the javelin is that it was won by the winning throw that we saw earlier.'

'Alan Pascoe could have won the gold, but he simply ran out of time.'

'Charlie Speeding believes in an even pace and hopes to run the second part of the race faster than the first.'

'It's a battle with himself and with the ticking finger of the clock.'
'And the line-up for the final of the women's 400 metres hurdles includes three Russians, two East Europeans, a Pole, a Swede and a Frenchman.'

'There's going to be a real ding-dong when the bell goes.'

'You've got to hand it to Gonzalez, once he saw it was possible, he saw his chance and made it possible.'

'He's even smaller in real life than he is on the track.'

'Dusty Hare kicked 19 of the 17 points.'

'Morceli has the four fastest 1,500-metre times ever. And all those times are at 1,500 metres.'

'He won the bronze medal in the 1976 Olympics, so he is used to being out in front.'

'There'll only be one winner in every sense of the word.'

'Lillian Board's great strength is her great strength.'

It would have been a tragedy of monumental proportions if Coleman's unique style had been denied to football. Thankfully, it was not and the following pay testimony to the great man's work in the beautiful game.

'Kevin Reeves, who's just turned 22, proving that an ill wind blows nobody any good.'

'Don't tell those coming in the final result of the fantastic match, but let's just have another look at Italy's winning goal.'

'On this 101st cup final day, there are just two teams left.'

'Some names to look forward to – perhaps in the future.'
'The pace of this match is really accelerating, by which I mean it is getting faster all the time.'

'The ball has broken 50–50 for Keegan.'

'Both of the Villa scorers – Withe and Mortimer – were born in Liverpool, as was the Villa manager – Ron Saunders – who was born in Birkenhead.'

'Manchester United are buzzing around the goalmouth like a lot of red bottles.'

'For those of you watching who do not have television sets, live commentary is on Radio 2.'

'If that had gone in, it would have been a goal.'

'Billy Hughes is like electricity: very sharp.'

'He is a whole-hearted player.'

> *On Asa Hartford, who has a hole-in-the-heart condition*

I WISH I HADN'T SAID THAT

One of the hazards of live broadcasting is that on-air blunders cannot be edited out. Football commentators and pundits have created mirth and mayhem down the years when their brains and mouths have not been as well connected as might have been desired. As the following quotes indicate, our lives have been enriched by the verbal mishaps of these mic-mincers, who are the true inheritors of the legacy of David Coleman.

'Julian Dicks is everywhere. It's like they've got eleven Dicks on the field.'

> *Metro Radio commentator*

'The scoreline didn't really reflect the outcome.'

> *Tony Gubba*

'Their away record is instantly forgettable. The 5–1 defeat and 7–0 defeat spring to mind.'

> *Ian Payne*

'The Dutch look like a huge jar of marmalade.'

> *Barry Davies*

'Wilkins sends an inch-perfect pass to no one in particular.'

> *Bryon Butler*

'It really needed the blink of an eyelid, otherwise you would have missed it.'

> *Peter Jones*

'United have a very experienced bench, which they may want to play to turn the tide of the match.'

Bryon Butler

'But the ball was going all the way, right away, eventually.'

Archie McPherson

'Lukic saved with his foot, which is all part of the goalkeeper's arm.'

Barry Davies

'It could be bad news for Andy Sinton. His knee is locked up in the dressing-room.'

George Gavin

'And now that we have the formalities over, we'll have the national anthems.'

Brian Moore

'Last week's match was a real game of cat and dog.'

John Aldridge

'Ian Rush unleashed his left foot and it hit the back of the net.'

Mike England

'Manchester City's Shaun Wright-Phillips, who is, of course, Ian Wright's son. He doesn't look anything like him, though.'

BBC Five Live commentator. Wright-Phillips is adopted

'Glenn Hoddle hasn't been the Hoddle we know. Neither has Bryan Robson.'

Gary Newbon

'Sporting Lisbon in their green and white hoops, looking like a team of zebras.'

Peter Jones

'Hodge scored for Forest after only 22 seconds, totally against the run of play.'

Peter Lorenzo

'If a week's a long time in politics it is an equinox in football.'

Stuart Hall

'And now for the goals from Carrow Road, where the game ended 0–0.'

Elton Welsby

'Chesterfield 1, Chester 1. Another score draw there in that local derby.'

Desmond Lynam

'With the very last kick of the game, Bobby McDonald scored with a header.'

Alan Parry

'It looks like something you'd reject for the kitchen curtains.'

Brian Moore on Arsenal's away strip in 1993

'If there's a goal now, I'll eat my hat.'

BBC radio commentator Tommy Woodruff during the 1938 FA Cup final. There was and he did (or at least he ate a cake modelled on it).

'It's slightly alarming the way Manchester United decapitated against Stuttgart.'

Mark Lawrenson

'He will probably wake up after having sleepless nights thinking about that one.'

Alan Parry

'If you had a linesman on each side of the pitch, in both halves you'd have nearly four.'

Robbie Earle

'After a goalless first half, the score at half-time is 0–0.'

Brian Moore

'The ageless Teddy Sheringham, 37 now.'

Tony Gubba

'Obviously, for Scunthorpe it would be a nice scalp to put Wimbledon on their bottoms.'

Dave Bassett

'Wayne Clarke, one of the famous Clarke family, and he's one of them, of course.'

Brian Moore

'He went down like a sack of potatoes, then made a meal of it.'

Trevor Brooking

'I felt a lump in my mouth as the ball went in.'

Terry Venables

'Being naturally right-footed, he doesn't often chance his arm with his left foot.'

Trevor Brooking

'Here's Brian Flynn. His official height is five feet five and he doesn't look much taller than that.'

Alan Green

'He signals to the bench with his groin.'

Mark Bright

'The shot brought back memories of Peter Lorimer . . . even though he's not dead yet.'

Chris Kamara

TODAY FM'S MATT COOPER: 'Is there any chance that Charlton could beat Chelsea?'

TONY CASCARINO: 'In a word, I don't think so.'

'Burton just couldn't lose tonight. Except that they did.'

Ian Wright

'Football today would certainly not be the same if it had not existed.'

Elton Welsby

'The Austrians are wearing the dark-black socks.'

Barry Davies

'The players with the wind will have to control it a lot more.'

Jack Charlton

'He'll give it everything he's got, but he's got nothing left to give.'

Ian St John

'Scotland were unlucky not to get another penalty like the one that wasn't given in the first half.'

Jimmy Hill

'Peter Ward has become a new man, just like his old self.'

Jim Rosenthal

'I'm sure that Ron Greenwood will hope that by the time England get to Spain, Kevin Keegan will have got his misses out of his system.'

Gerald Sinstadt, hoping that Keegan will be able to put his mistakes, rather than his marriage, behind him in sunny Spain

'It's one of the greatest goals ever, but I'm surprised that people are talking about it being the goal of the season.'

Andy Gray

'We are now in the middle of the centre of the first half.'

David Pleat

'It's an end-of-season curtain raiser.'

Peter Withe

'Charlie George was one of Arsenal's all-time great players. A lot of people might not agree with that, but I personally do.'

Jimmy Greaves

EL TEL

While for the most part football pundits cause mirth unintentionally, sometimes they score with a well-prepared line such as Terry Venables' exclamation, 'The 'Ungarians 'ave been goulashed!'

A NO-BRAINER

A man finds out that he has a brain tumour and it's so large that they have to do a brain transplant. His doctor gives him a choice of available brains. There's a jar of rocket scientists' brains for £100 pounds an ounce, a jar of dentists' brains for £150 pounds an ounce and a jar of football pundits' brains for £100,000 pounds an ounce.

The outraged patient says, 'This is a rip-off! How come the football pundits' brains are so damned expensive?'

The doctor replies, 'Do you know how many football pundits it takes to get an ounce of brains?'

A PARABLE

Into every pundit's life some rain must fall. When it's your job to give your opinion on poor performances and controversial decisions, you're not always going to be popular. The likes of Alan Hansen would do well to bear in mind the story of the football analyst, the donkey and the bridge.

A football analyst and his son were taking their donkey to the fair. The man was walking with the donkey and his son was up on the animal's back. A passer-by said, 'Isn't it a disgrace to see that poor man walking and the young fellow up on the donkey having an easy time. He should walk and let his poor father have a rest.'

So the boy dismounted and the father took his place. A mile later, they met another man who said, 'Isn't it a disgrace to have that boy walking while his father takes it easy. You should both get up on the donkey's back.'

They duly did, but a little further along they met an enraged woman who screamed, 'How cruel it is to have two healthy men up on that poor donkey's back. The two of you should get down and carry the donkey.'

Again they did as they were told, but as they walked over a bridge, the donkey fell into the river and drowned.

The moral of the story is that if you're an analyst and you're trying to please everyone, you might as well kiss your ass goodbye.

STRAIGHT TALKING

Having been a great player in the past doesn't necessarily make you an entertaining pundit. A good example of this is Sir Bobby Charlton. He was in great demand by broadcasters. However, he was perhaps too nice a guy. He rarely had a bad word to say about anybody and as a result his comments could be quite bland. In marked contrast, his brother Jack was fun to watch because he always gave forthright answers. A good example of this was when he was assessing the Holland–Germany game on ITV during the 1990 World Cup. Frank Rijkaard and Rudi Völler had had what is called in football parlance 'a bust-up' and Rijkaard had spat at his opponent. Jack was asked what he would have done if Rijkaard had done that to him. Without blinking an eye, Big Jack replied, 'I'd have chinned him.'

ENGLAND EXPECTS

Few things excite the English media more than the fate of the national team. Sometimes it seems that they struggle to accept the evidence of their own eyes when England are defeated. Certainly, Dickie Davies seemed to be having difficulty with the concept when he said, 'England were beaten in the sense that they lost.' However, when England lose spectacularly, the print media are not found wanting. As the following responses show, Graham Taylor's team got a particularly rough ride.

'Swedes 2, Turnips 1'

> The Sun's *headline after Sweden's win over England in 1992*

'England were losing to a mountain-top. Ben Nevis 1, the Turnips 0.'

> *Joe Lovejoy in* The Independent *on England's 1993 World Cup qualifier against San Marino, in which the minnows went ahead after nine seconds*

'This is a goal, this is a ball. Put one in the other and advance.'

> The *Daily Mirror's advice to England*

'Yanks 2, Planks 0'

> The Sun *after England lost to the United States in 1993*

'Norse Manure'

> The *Daily Mirror's verdict after Norway beat England, 1993*

A GRAVE MATTER

A busload of football pundits were driving down a country road when all of a sudden the bus ran off the road and crashed into a tree in an old farmer's field. The farmer saw what happened and went over to investigate. He then proceeded to dig a big hole and bury the pundits.

A few days later, the local sergeant saw the crashed bus and asked the farmer where all the pundits had gone. The old farmer said he had buried them. The officer then asked, 'So they were all dead?'

The old farmer replied, 'Well, some of them said they weren't, but, you know, them pundits talk rubbish.'

SCHOOL REUNION

A Sky Sports pundit went to visit his old school. He asked the pupils if anyone could give him an example of a tragedy. One boy stood up and offered the suggestion, 'If my best friend who lives next door was playing in the street when a car came along and killed him, that would be a tragedy.'

'No,' said the pundit, 'That would be an *accident*.'

Another boy raised his hand. 'If a school bus carrying 50 children drove off a cliff, killing everybody involved . . . that would be a tragedy.'

'I'm afraid not,' he explained. 'That is what we would call a *great loss*.'

The room was silent; none of the other children volunteered anything. 'What?' asked the pundit. 'Is there no one here who can give me an example of a tragedy?'

Finally, a boy at the back raised his hand. 'If an aeroplane carrying the Sky Sports team was blown up by a bomb, that would be a tragedy.'

'Wonderful. Marvellous. And can you tell me why that would be a tragedy?'

'Well,' said the boy, 'because it wouldn't be an accident, and it certainly would be no great loss.'

SECOND PLACE

When Harold Macmillan became Prime Minister in 1957, his appointment was relegated to the second story in his local newspaper in Sussex. The top story was a report about a Brighton and Hove Albion football match. Macmillan kept the cutting on his desk at No. 10 in order, in his own words, 'to prevent myself indulging in the impulse towards self-importance'.

THE LAST WORD

Most commentary induces a state of 'déjà moo' – the feeling that you've heard this bull before. Every now and again, however, the pundits come out with something memorably ill-judged.

'With 8 or 10 minutes to go, they were able to bring Nicky Butt back and give him 15 to 20 minutes.'

Niall Quinn

'You felt that was the sort of game that needed a goal to break the deadlock.'

BBC Radio 5 Live's Ron Jones

'So, Tim, without naming names, who was the best centre-half you ever played behind?'

Rob McCaffrey

'Steve McCall is trying to thread a needle through a haystack here.'

Mark Bright

'One–nil is not a winning score, by any means.'

BBC Radio Derby's Ian Hall

'It's all square at the Oval.'

BBC Northern Ireland commentator

'They've forced them into a lot of unforced errors.'

Steve Claridge

'I expect Chelsea to make a world-record signing in the near distant future.'

Tony Cascarino

'He has broken his left leg, which is a real kick in the teeth for him.'

> BBC Radio 5 Live's Luke Harvey

'It was a bit of a surprise and yet I shouldn't have been surprised, because I was a bit surprised he was going to go in the first place.'

> Terry Venables on Robbie Fowler's proposed move to Manchester City from Leeds United in 2003

'Often the most vulnerable area for goalies is between their legs.'

> Andy Gray

'You've got to believe you'll win, and I believe we'll win the World Cup till the final whistle blows and we're knocked out.'

> Peter Shilton

'To play Holland, you have to play the Dutch.'

> Ruud Gullit

'This is going to be a very long 30 minutes with 26 minutes left to go.'

> Brian Moore

'It's only at the point of climax that there's a ripple of noise.'

> Jon Champion

'It's an incredible rise to stardom. At 17, you're more likely to get a call from Michael Jackson than Sven-Göran Eriksson.'

> Channel 4's Derek McGovern on Wayne Rooney's first call-up to the English squad

'Well, Manchester Uni– I mean, Manchester City are in action tonight. Sorry, I almost said Manchester United there – a bit of a fraudulent slip.'

> Talksport's Bill Young

CALLER TO TALKSPORT: 'First of all, can you wish me a happy 40th birthday?'

IAN WRIGHT: 'And how old are you?'

'He's done nothing wrong, but his movement's not great and his distribution's been poor.'

Alan Mullery

'Never mind leaping like a salmon, Jeff, he leaps like a goldfish.'

Rodney Marsh

'It is one of those goals that's invariably a goal.'

Denis Law

'You only get one opportunity of an England debut.'

Alan Shearer

'Fifty-two thousand people here at Maine Road tonight, but my goodness me, it seems like fifty thousand.'

Byron Butler

'The run of the ball is not in our court at the moment.'

Phil Neal

'Oh, he had an eternity to play that ball, but he took too long over it.'

Martin Tyler

'A win tonight is the minimum City must achieve.'

Alan Parry

10

SIR BOBBY

'We didn't underestimate them. They were just a lot better than we thought.'

Bobby Robson on the
Cameroon team in 1990

As this book was being completed, the sad news broke of the death of Sir Bobby Robson after a brave battle against lung cancer, during which his foundation raised £1.6 million towards research into the disease. Sir Bobby was a national treasure. Of all the tributes paid to him, perhaps the most touching was Paul Gascoigne's: 'Bobby was like my second dad. I can't describe how much he meant to me. I'm numb.' This chapter is offered as a small tribute to a great man.

BLACK-AND-WHITE KNIGHT

On being made Sir Bobby in 2002, Robson quipped, 'I've always enjoyed a night on the town in Newcastle – now you could say I am a knight of the toon.'

IT COULD BE WORSE

Robson was perhaps one of football's least cynical characters and always seemed able to see the good in a situation, no matter what: 'When we had our recent depressing run and did not win for seven matches, five of them were away from home. And we actually lost the two home games against Middlesbrough and Manchester City. So while things were bleak, they looked a lot bleaker than they really were.' On the other hand, he could possibly have set his sights a little higher at times: 'We shall set out to be as positive as possible and look to pick up a point.'

BOBBY BAMBOOZLES

Guardian football correspondent David Lacey observed of Bobby Robson: 'His natural expression is that of a man who fears he might have left the gas on.' That might be a little harsh; what cannot be disputed, however, is that some of Sir Bobby's comments had a unique power to bewilder and bemuse. Here's a selection of my favourite Bobbyisms.

'We're flying on Concorde. That'll shorten the distance. That's self-explanatory.'

'Some of the goals were good, some of the goals were sceptical.'

'I do want to play the long ball and I do want to play the short ball. I think long and short balls is what football is all about.'

'We've got nothing to lose, and there's no point losing this game.'

'Gary Speed has been absolutely massive for me . . . his influence on the team cannot be underestimated.'

'The first ninety minutes are the most important.'

'We had the game won and then all of a sudden we lost it.'

On Kevin Sheedy's equaliser for Ireland
against England in Italia '90

'The last thing I want to do now is win something for the fantastic supporters in Newcastle.'

'With Maradona, even Arsenal would have won it [the 1986 World Cup].'

'We can't replace Gary Speed. Where do you get an experienced player like him with a left foot and a head?'

'Home advantage gives you an advantage.'

'He's very fast and if he gets a yard ahead of himself, nobody will catch him.'

'Well, we got nine and you can't score more than that.'

'I'd say he's the best in Europe if you put me on the fence.'

'Tottenham have impressed me. They haven't thrown in the towel even though they have been under the gun.'

'I played cricket for my local village. It was 40 overs per side, and the team that had the most runs won. It was that sort of football.'

'There will be a game where somebody scores more than Brazil and that might be the game that they lose.'

'We don't want our players to be monks; we want them to be football players, because a monk doesn't play football at this level.'

THE NAME OF THE GAME

As a manager, Robson had a reputation for being less than reliably accurate when it came to players' names. He is said to have called Laurent Robert 'Lauren Bacall' on at least one occasion, and Bryan Robson remembers that when he was in the England squad he was once greeted with, 'Morning, Bobby,' to which he helpfully replied, 'No, boss, you're Bobby, I'm Bryan.'

According to legend, Foluwashola Ameobi, who was battling for his place in the first team with Carl Cort at Newcastle under Robson, was asked in an interview about his long name. The conversation supposedly went as follows.

JOURNALIST: 'Do you have a nickname?'
AMEOBI: 'No, not really.'
JOURNALIST: 'What do the lads call you?'
AMEOBI: 'Shola.'
JOURNALIST: 'So what does Bobby Robson call you?'
AMEOBI: 'Carl Cort.'

ON AUTOPILOT

According to one (possibly apocryphal) story about Sir Bobby, he was coming to the end of a long session signing his autobiography in a Newcastle bookshop when a young Magpies fan arrived at the front of the queue.

Bobby asked, 'Who should I sign it to?'

The fan replied, 'Could you make it out to Michael?'

'No problem, son.'

Politely, the boy said, 'You must have signed an awful lot today, then?'

Bobby replied, 'Hundreds son, hundreds and hundreds!'

When the boy looked at the inscription, it read: 'Best wishes to Michael, from Bobby Hundreds.'

INDIVIDUAL FLAIR

In the course of a long career as both manager and pundit, Bobby made some classic comments on players. These are my top five.

1. 'Laurent Robert said I was picking the wrong team. At the time, I was, because he was in it.'

2. 'When Gazza was dribbling, he used to go through a minefield with his arm, a bit like you go through a supermarket.'

3. 'He's going a bit thin on top and in this heat it can happen that he loses his temper a bit quicker than usual.'

> *Sir Bobby claims that Ray Wilkins was sent off in the 1986 World Cup because of baldness*

4. 'It wasn't the hand of God. It was the hand of a rascal.'

> *On the infamous Maradona goal at the 1986 World Cup*

5. 'Everton will want to sedate Wayne Rooney and keep the boy calm, and that is the right thing to do.'

11

THE GLOBAL GAME

'The World Cup is truly an international event.'

John Motson

Such has been the influx of foreign players into the top flight of English football that when none of the home countries qualified for Euro 2008, it was waspishly observed that watching the tournament would be pretty much the same as watching the Premiership. Of course, there has also been traffic in the other direction, though am I the only one to find Steve McManaman's 2003 comment a bit odd? 'Coming to Manchester City, if anything, is more exciting than being at Real Madrid.'

TURKISH DELIGHT

After he moved from Aberdeen to Besiktas in Turkey, the Norwegian striker Arild Stavrum received an unexpected surprise: 'Tired after practice, I had a shower. I put a lot of soap on and after opening my eyes I realised that I was the only naked man among ten Turks wearing shorts. Then a German entered the shower and I was happy. I doubt that Elton John would be happier than me to see a naked young man.'

WITH FRIENDS LIKE THESE

Sampdoria's Antonio Cassano had a cool relationship with his teammate Gabriel Batistuta. In his autobiography, he claimed: 'One day at training we were queuing at the bar, he arrived and pushed in front of me. We were both getting a macchiato. So I stuck a finger up my nose and stirred his drink with it, like it was a spoon.'

In the circumstances, Fabio Capello, his manager at Roma and Real Madrid, must have felt he got away lightly. They had an even more fractious relationship, but Cassano only said to him, 'You're a shit. You are faker than Monopoly money.'

SPECIAL ONES

In recent years, there's been a huge rise in the number of Continental managers working in British football, many of them fascinating characters, and none more so than former Chelsea gaffer José Mourinho. His barbed comments about his managerial opponents are famous. My top five are:

1. 'I think he is one of these people who is a voyeur. He likes to watch other people. There are some guys who, when they are at home, have a big telescope to see what happens in other families. He speaks, speaks, speaks about Chelsea.'

    Getting agitated about Arsène Wenger
    expressing his views on the Blues in 2005. Mourinho later
    apologised for his comments.

2. 'Arsenal are a unique team. Their coach hasn't won anything for years, but he's still an idol.'

    A back-handed compliment for Wenger in 2008

3. 'I've won a lot in my career. He has won a Super Cup and another little cup. Probably he needs to change mentality, but maybe he is too old to do it.'

    Mourinho is charm itself on Claudio Ranieri

4. 'Maybe in the philosophy of a loser this was a great season.'

A dispassionate assessment of his
successor at Chelsea, Avram Grant

5. 'I saw their players and manager go for a lap of honour after losing to us in their last home game. In Portugal, if you do this, they throw bottles at you!'

On Sir Alex Ferguson and Man United in 2005

IN THE POST

Despite his commitment to Inter Milan, Mourinho retains a close friendship with many of his former Chelsea players. He was distraught when his good mate John Terry missed a penalty that cost Chelsea the Champions League final in 2008. José wrote him a sympathetic letter, but tragically it missed the post.

YOU CAN HANDLE THE TRUTH

Before the Special One, Chelsea were managed by Tinkerman Claudio Ranieri. One of the things that endeared him to the fans was his honesty. What other Premiership manager would admit that he gets grief from his mother over team selection: 'When I don't put Damien in the squad, my mother, who's 84, says, "Why?" She kills me. That's true.' However, the most striking illustration of his frankness came when he said, 'The Stamford Bridge pitch is shit, yes, very shit. But it OK. It *our* shit.' Mourinho's take on the playing surface was more philosophical: 'Sometimes you see beautiful people with no brains, but you see ugly people who are intelligent scientists. Our pitch is like that. From the top it's a disgrace, but the ball rolls at normal speed.'

WHEN IN BARNSLEY

It's not always easy for players from the Continent to adjust
to the English way of life. When Macedonian striker Gjorgji
Hristov moved to the Premiership in 1997, he made himself
unpopular in Barnsley by moaning in a magazine interview
back home: 'I'm finding it difficult to find a girlfriend in
Barnsley. The local girls are far uglier than the ones back in
Belgrade or Skopje. Our women are much prettier. Besides,
they don't drink as much beer as the Barnsley girls, which is
something I don't like at all.'

FROM RUSSIA WITH LOVE

So you don't think international history impacts on football?
Well, maybe not all that often, but one urban myth suggests
otherwise. According to legend, 'the Russian linesman' at the
1966 World Cup final, Tofik Bakhramov of Azerbaijan, when
asked on his deathbed how he could have been sure that the
controversial third goal, which hit the crossbar and bounced
straight down, had crossed the line, answered with one word:
'Stalingrad.'

THE KAISER CHIEF

One of the great European footballers was Franz Beckenbauer.
'Der Kaiser', who captained West Germany to the 1974 World
Cup and managed them to the World Cup in 1990, was asked
how he always seemed to get from A to B faster than his
opponent, even though his opponent was invariably quicker.
He replied, 'I don't start from A.'

THE MEAT IN THE SANDWICH

From Romania comes a story that provides a refreshing
antidote to the over-inflated fees and hype of the Premiership,
Serie A and La Liga. In 2006, fourth-division Romanian
football team Regal Hornia secured the services of Marius

Cioara from second-division UT Arad by offering a transfer fee of 15 kg of pork sausages. Regal were said to be confident that the sacrifice of a week's sausage allowance would be worth it, but it turned out not to be such a great deal after all. The defender retired a day later saying he could not face any more meat-related taunts, and complaining, 'They were joking I would have got more from the Germans and making sausage jokes.'

THE FRENCH CONNECTION

One of the greatest ever foreign players in the Premier League was Eric Cantona. When he first moved to England to play for Leeds United, Cantona struggled with culture shock. For example, it took him a few years to figure out the English class system. Of course, it's fairly simple, really. You are part of the upper class when your name is written in *Debrett's Peerage*; part of the middle class when your name is written on your office door; and part of the lower class when your name is written on a badge on your shirt.

He certainly had some nice things to say about his new home, though, once declaring: 'In England everything is beautiful. The stadiums are beautiful, the atmosphere is beautiful, the cops on horseback are beautiful. The crowds respect you.'

Cantona was a lot more cerebral than most footballers, given to making declarations such as, 'There is nothing more paradoxical nor more breathtaking than a goal in front of a crowd which is waiting for it,' and 'The penalty is either happiness or sadness, nothing in between.'

JUST LIKE A WOMAN

Even for a renowned international footballer, Cantona had a lot of flair, and he was a glamorous figure in the English game. He was just so . . . French. Take, for example, his penchant for romantic metaphors. On his move to Manchester United, he said: 'I leave when I need to change. It's like being with a woman. If you get to the point when you've got nothing left to say to her, you leave. Or else you stop being good together.'

How very Gallic. When he left the game altogether to become an actor, he compared that to the end of a relationship, too – 'It is like when you leave a woman and you don't cry when she goes off with someone else' – but also gave the less traditional board-game simile a whirl: 'The danger with games is that you can get tired of them. That's why I swapped soccer for cinema in the way a child takes up playing Cluedo when he is sick of Monopoly.'

A JACKIE CHAN MOMENT

Cantona's most infamous moment was when, having been sent off during a match at Crystal Palace, he launched a kung fu kick at an abusive home fan on his way to the tunnel. The incident divided the public, with Palace fans taking the view that it was a case of the shit hitting the fan. The saga spawned some great quotes.

'When the seagulls follow the trawler, it is because they think sardines will be thrown into the sea.'

Cantona's enigmatic pronouncement, his only words at the press conference about the incident

'Sharp are currently working on bringing 3D TV into your living rooms. Mr Koshima hopes it will be so realistic that viewers will have to duck when Eric Cantona takes a shot.'

Dramatic irony courtesy of a press release issued by Manchester United's sponsors days before the Crystal Palace match

'1966 was a great year for English football. Eric was born.'

Nike slogan

'1995 was a great year for English football. Eric was banned.'

T-shirt slogan

'If a Frenchman goes on about seagulls, trawlers and sardines, he's called a philosopher. I'd just be called a short Scottish bum talking crap.'

Gordon Strachan. Life is so unfair.

'If somebody in the crowd spits at you, you've just got to swallow it.'

Hygienic advice from Gary Lineker

'I don't think we should pay too much heed to rumours that his next acting role will be in a new TV sitcom called *One Foot in the Crowd*.'

Film critic Barry Norman

'My best moment? I have a lot of good moments but the one I prefer is when I kicked the hooligan.'

Eric Cantona

'My lawyer and the officials wanted me to speak. So I just said that. It was nothing; it did not mean anything. I could have said, "The curtains are pink, but I love them."'

The final word on his trawlers and sardines pronouncement

ERIC THE PHILOSOPHER

Known to the fans as 'King Eric', and sometimes even 'God', there's no doubt that Cantona was an exceptional player. But off the pitch he could sometimes come across as – how can I put this? – just a little bit pretentious.

'I will never find any difference between Pelé's pass to Carlos Alberto in the final of the 1970 World Cup and the poetry of the young Rimbaud.'

'Peaks of happiness and depths of pain – just like the chain of mountains in the Alps where I am going to rest and paint.'

Describing the past season in 1993

'I've read a lot of Socrates on Page 3 of *The Sun*.'

'Our mission was to interpret *The Magic Flute*, every Saturday.'

On playing for Montpellier FC

BON MOT

English football interviewers, accustomed to a diet of 'the lads gave it 110 per cent' clichés from footballers, sometimes appeared to find Cantona's dashing, enigmatic persona a bit unsettling, ironically resulting in some truly underwhelming exchanges, such as the following with a doyen of ITV football coverage.

ELTON WELSBY: '*Magnifique*, Eric.'

ERIC CANTONA: 'Oh, do you speak French?'

ELTON WELSBY: '*Non*.'

QUOTE UNQUOTE

They may often have a better command of the language than most native speakers in the game, but players and managers from foreign climes have still managed to come out with a lot of rubbish over the years. And there's nothing like a trip abroad to get a commentator overexcited. The following are some of the best examples of international football foot-in-mouth syndrome.

'Lord Nelson, Lord Beaverbrook, Sir Winston Churchill, Sir Anthony Eden, Clement Attlee, Henry Cooper, Lady Diana ... Maggie Thatcher – can you hear me, Maggie Thatcher? Your boys took a hell of a beating!'

Norwegian commentator Bjorge Lillelien after Norway's shock victory over England in a World Cup qualifier in 1981

'You only sing when you're whaling.'

> *Scottish fans' chant at Norwegian fans*
> *during the 1998 World Cup finals*

'Alcoholism v. Communism'

> *Banner at Scotland v. the USSR in 1982*

'Tommy Coyne. Sharper than Jimmy Hill's chin.'

> *Banner at Ireland v. Italy in USA '94*

'The European Cup is 17 lb of silver and it's worth its weight in gold.'

> *Brian Moore*

'"Football's coming home," the English fans sang in Euro '96. And it was. To Germany.'

> *Joseph O'Connor*

'The game in Romania was a game we should have won. We lost it because we thought we were going to win it. But then again, I thought there was no way we were going to get a result there.'

> *Jack Charlton, sounding slightly muddled*
> *after Ireland's defeat by Bulgaria in 1987*

'Only if there is an outbreak of bubonic plague.'

> *Giovanni Trapattoni pulled no punches when asked if he planned*
> *to pick Paolo Di Canio for the Italian World Cup side in 2004*

'Germany are probably, unarguably, undisputed champions of Europe.'

> *Bryan Hamilton*

'Someone asked me last week if I missed the Villa. I said, "No, I live in one."'

> *David Platt following his transfer from*
> *Aston Villa to Bari in 1991*

'Like a woman on her wedding day – nervous, out of position and hoping everything would soon be over so she could go up to the bedroom.'

> Spanish newspaper Marca *on a Fabien Barthez performance against Real Madrid*

'Do you remember when we played in Spain in the Anglo–Italian?'

> *Shaun Newton*

CANADIAN REPORTER: 'How will the Mexican goalkeeper approach this game, given what's happened to him this week?'

FORMER IPSWICH GOALIE CRAIG FORREST: 'Well, his father passed away on Thursday. He'll be disappointed with that.'

'Switzerland seem the hungrier, while Ireland seem prepared to wait for room service.'

> *George Hamilton*

'For a game played in Cologne, that stank.'

> *Mark Lawrenson after Switzerland v. Ukraine in 2006*

'Glen Johnson is an England international in the making. Although he has already played for England.'

> *Sky Sports' Tony Gale*

'This is cup football now, it's all one-off games – and we have two of them against Valencia.'

> *Rio Ferdinand*

'My only problem seems to be with Italian breakfasts. No matter how much money you've got, you can't get Rice Krispies.'

> *Luther Blissett on his move to the Continent*

'Football is a game of twenty-two players and one football where Germany always win on penalties.'

Gary Lineker

'Those who consider me slow don't know me very well, because I've never been quick.'

Laurent Blanc

'Juninho will only need to learn three words of English: pound, thank you and bye bye.'

Norwegian footballer Jan Aage Fjortoft on Juninho's transfer to Middlesbrough in 1995

'I couldn't settle in Italy. It was like living in a foreign country.'

Attributed to Ian Rush

'Samassi Abou don't speak the English too good.'

Harry Redknapp

'It's best that I hide my real personality. I cannot tell you what it is because I don't want to go to prison.'

A startling admission from Gianfranco Zola

'I don't have any. I was sent to bed before the matches started.'

Michael Owen on his memories of the 1990 World Cup

'Like so many of the current Chelsea team, Zola is unique.'

Barry Venison

'I'd like to play for an Italian club, like Barcelona.'

Mark Draper

'The news from Guadalajara, where the temperature is 96 degrees, is that Falcão is warming up.'

Brian Moore

'Are you from Australia? What's happening in *Neighbours*?'

Ireland's Jason McAteer, talking to a journalist at a press conference during the 1994 World Cup

'[Liam] Brady's been playing inside Platini's shorts all night.'

RTÉ commentator Jimmy Magee

'I have Gary Lineker's shirt up in my hotel room, and it's only stopped moving now.'

Mick McCarthy, the day after Ireland's win against England in 1988

REPORTER: 'Would you like to leave England with an honorary knighthood?'

SVEN GÖRAN-ERIKSSON: 'I would like to leave alive.'

'A big stork (maybe with avian flu) called Peter Crouch, whose football sounds as bad as his name and whose photos can't be published even in a family scrapbook.'

Italian newspaper La Repubblica

'I have black, Gypsy and Japanese friends, including one whose job it is to determine the sex of poultry.'

Spanish coach Luis Aragonés. Good for him.

'They might do a Greece [win a major tournament against all the odds]. Like Greece did.'

Terry Butcher

'If Brazil are the best team in the world, then I am Geri Halliwell.'

Elton John

'When it comes to taking penalties, England are the world's idiots.'

German paper Bild am Sonntag

'It looks like England have beaten Sweden for the first time in 38 years.'

Clive Tyldesley, seconds before Sweden equalised

'Kasey Keller is a very educated man – he wears spectacles off the pitch.'

John Helm

'He's not getting any older.'

Peter Schmeichel explaining why Nicky Butt should leave Manchester United in 2003

'Our hopes could be handicapped by us not knowing how to defend.'

Robert Pirès on Arsenal's Champions League chances, 2003

'The supporters are like a woman who you have to keep happy every day.'

Ronaldo on why Real Madrid always try to play entertaining football

'For me pressure is bird flu. I am feeling a lot of pressure with the swan in Scotland. I am serious. You are laughing but I am serious. I am more scared of the bird flu than football. What is football compared with life? A swan with bird flu, for me, that is the drama of the last two days. I have to buy some masks and stuff. I am serious. Maybe for my team as well.'

José Mourinho in 2006. Wonder how he feels about swine flu?

'I'm not a betting man – but I bet you Italy will win.'

Graham Taylor

'Who is Souleymane Diawara? If he went to play in Saudi Arabia, people would ask, "What kind of ketchup is that?"'

El Hadji Diouf on his Senegal teammate

OLIVER'S TWIST

Every cloud has a silver lining. During the 2002 World Cup final, the German goalkeeper Oliver Kahn was distraught when he made a howler that allowed Brazil's Ronaldo to tap the ball into the net for the opening goal. So often were the heartbreaking scenes from the match replayed on television that Kahn became a tragic hero, winning the love of the Far Eastern fans. He became a major celebrity in Asia, was signed to a multimillion-dollar advertising deal and is set to star in a reality TV show in China.

ONE ON ONE

When José Antonio Reyes came to London to play for Arsenal, he found a large number of gnomes in the garden of his new home. Resourcefully, he set up the two largest ones as goalposts and used several others dotted around the garden as a makeshift dribbling course. 'I like to work out with the gnomes,' said Reyes. Fair enough, you might think, but he followed that up with a somewhat more baffling admission: 'Sometimes I even play goalkeeper.'

I DON'T LOVE THE SOUND OF BREAKING GLASS

In 2004, Brazilian star Ronaldinho was filming a TV advert, with the beautiful cathedral of Santiago de Compostela as a backdrop. At one point, the director asked him to perform a scissor kick, striking the ball as hard as he could. Ronaldinho gave it his best but smashed a window in the cathedral's Pórtico de la Gloria. Luckily for player and director, the smashed pane was a modern addition rather than one of the original medieval ones.

EXIT STRATEGY

Manchester United are in Moscow for the 2008 Champions League, and Alex Ferguson notices that Cristiano Ronaldo is missing when the team assemble in the hotel foyer. He calls the star's room, wondering what's happened to him. Ronaldo tells him he can't get out.

'Why not?' Ferguson demands.

Ronaldo replies, 'There are only three doors in here. One is the bathroom, one is the cupboard and one has a sign on it that says, "Do not disturb".'

STAR TREK

In 2003, the mayor of Brazilian town Bocaiuva do Sul, Elcio Berti, told the press that he had cancelled a planned landing by an alien craft during an international between Brazil and Peru. Why? He told journalists, 'I cancelled the landing because I was worried they might abduct one of the Brazilian footballers.'

ANYTHING YOU CAN DO, WE CAN DO BETTER

When Chelsea were taken over by Russian multimillionaire Roman Abramovich, they were immediately renamed Chelski by the press. Armed with their new Russian roubles, they spent money on new players as if it was going out of fashion. It seemed as if any time a big-money player became available, Chelski were in like a flash, topping everybody else's bid.

This led to a story about Abramovich being chauffeur-driven to the opening game of the season. Abramovich is a bit preoccupied, so when news comes through on the radio that the American government have offered $35 million for Saddam Hussein, he immediately gets on the phone to Chelsea's financial director and says, 'That guy the Americans want – let's offer $40 million for him.'

A QUESTION OF NATIONALITY

Steven Gerrard, Thierry Henry and Roman Abramovich
are looking at a painting of Adam and Eve frolicking in the
Garden of Eden.

'Look at their reserve, their calm,' muses Gerrard. 'They
must be British.'

'Nonsense,' Henry disagrees. 'They're naked, and so
beautiful. Clearly, they are French.'

'No clothes, no shelter,' Abramovich points out, 'they have
only an apple to eat, and they're being told this is paradise.
They are definitely Russian.'

12

ASPECTS OF LOVE

'As a child, I took my ball to bed with me, and she's my one true love. She's honest and has never betrayed me.'

Chelsea's Adrian Mutu in 2003

In today's media-saturated world, gossip about a football player is at least as likely to concern bedroom activity as transfer activity. From footballers who have enjoyed visits to a brothel and the company of a 48-year-old grandmother known as 'the Auld Slapper' to those who have graced the pages of *OK!* with their glitzy £5-million weddings to the WAG of their choice . . . oh, hang on, that was the same player, wasn't it? Anyway, the point is that successful footballers, with ready supplies of cash and high profiles, have their pick of the ladies, and many players would agree with the famous quote from the western *Red River*: 'There are only two things more beautiful than a gun [read 'goal']: a Swiss watch or a woman from anywhere.'

Of course, love and sex have always been intimately intertwined with the beautiful game. Think, for example, of George Best's answer to Michael Parkinson when asked what was the nearest to kick-off he had made love to a woman: 'Half-time!' In the modern footballing era, though, it seems you can't get away from the subject. Even the *New Scientist* magazine got in on the act in 1999, reporting on a new condition – sexually acquired reactive arthritis – which footballers, so researchers discovered, are at greater risk of developing because of their promiscuity.

All this, of course, is not to say that true love never runs smoothly for the professional footballer, and they do have their romantic moments, as the case of Aston Villa and Reading midfielder Steve Sidwell shows. He went so far as to have the 100 words of his self-penned wedding vows, in which he pledges his undying love for his wife Krystell, tattooed on his back. The tattoo includes the words: 'Today I have not just found my partner or my soulmate but I have found my best friend. I will need and love you always. I love you.'

In July 2009, Cupid's arrow was also flying for Kolo Touré when he signed for Manchester City from Arsenal for £15 million. Asked about leaving Arsenal after seven years, Touré said, 'City showed they really wanted me. I always say when you love a woman and she gives you back the love, you are really happy. That's what Manchester City have done – given me the love. I am really delighted and I aim to give back the love as well.'

Even James Blunt could not match such sweet sentiments, and, like Wet Wet Wet, we can feel it in our fingers, we can feel it in our toes that love is all around in the football world.

EXPERT OPINIONS

Some players even feel the need to have a few attractive ladies around for the post-match analysis. Arsenal's Tomas Rosicky, along with five of his Czech teammates, was in the Hotel Praha at 5 a.m. comparing notes on the previous night's international fixture with six young ladies. The players were fined for excessive partying but all denied that they had slept with the women.

LET'S HAVE A CELEBRATION

If the ubiquitous kiss-and-tells are anything to go by, forwards have tended to replicate goal-scoring-style celebrations in the bedroom. One former love interest of Jermain Defoe's claimed that he enjoyed wearing her bra on his head and got into the mood by performing naked handstands.

HEARTS AND FLOWERS

On Valentine's Day 2008, Sheffield Wednesday's Rob Burch went on live daytime television to ask his beloved, a producer on ITV's *This Morning*, to become his lawfully wedded WAG. His girlfriend was delighted but somewhat gobsmacked, commenting, 'I wasn't expecting to see him until this afternoon. I've got a train ticket to Sheffield at half past two. I don't know what I'm going to do now.'

France coach Raymond Domenech wasn't so lucky when, live on TV directly after overseeing his side's inglorious exit from Euro 2008, he made a spontaneous and heartfelt declaration of his love for his long-term girlfriend and his intention to marry her. The French press derided the outburst as inappropriate and he later admitted that it had been 'an error'.

Rio Ferdinand proved to be equally demonstrative in March 2009, when he announced details of his upcoming marriage – including plans to have the rings flown in to the ceremony by an owl. Who knew romance flourished so imaginatively in the heart of the Manchester United defence?

AN INDECENT PROPOSAL

No matter how much you and your other half love your local team, you might be advised to reconsider if you're planning on popping the question at half-time. Couples who've got engaged at football matches have been treated to chants ranging from the relatively innocuous ('You don't know what you're doing!') to the downright mood-ruining ('We've all had your missus!').

ITALIAN STALLION

It's not just opportunistic young ladies who tell all about footballers in the bedroom. In his frank autobiography, hot-headed Sampdoria star Antonio Cassano boasted of his exploits. He wrote that 'four girlfriends in eleven years is a low number'. Well, yeah, you might think, certainly quite restrained for a footballer in his mid-20s. But he continued, 'I experienced some adventures. I slept with between 600 and 700 girls, 20 of whom were from the world of show business.'

He also claimed to have played great football shortly after having sex (even pointing to individual matches and filling readers in on the circumstances) and reminisced about a waiter he befriended when he was at Real Madrid. The man worked in the hotel where the squad stayed the night before home matches and helped Cassano to smuggle women out and food in: 'His job was to bring me three or four pastries after I had sex. He would bring them up the stairs, I would escort the woman to him and we would make an exchange.'

SEXY SEÑORITA

In the immediate build-up to the 2008 European Championships, the football media gave virtually no coverage to the tournament itself, so preoccupied was it with the soap opera of whether Real Madrid could prise away Cristiano Ronaldo from Manchester United. A major factor in the equation was said to be Ronaldo's then girlfriend, Spanish model Nereida Gallardo, who lived in Madrid. The *News of the World* breathlessly described her as 'a wild animal in bed'. As so often in top-flight football today, the hype amounted to not very much. After a few months, Ronaldo was still in Manchester (for the time being) and the tabloids were claiming that he had dumped Nereida by text.

A VEXED QUESTION

One of Ireland's leading writers, Joseph O'Connor, once posed the question, 'Is football better than sex?' He offered his own answer: 'At first glance, this might be considered a troublesome comparison, as the two activities are so remarkably different. I mean, one involves the complete engagement of the senses, wild abandonment, heart-stopping elation and, above all, orgasmic bliss. The other is sex.'

Opinions certainly vary. Lee Chapman took a balanced view, saying of scoring a goal, 'I wouldn't say it's better than sex, but it's a close call.' After winning the World Cup with Brazil, Ronaldo claimed that it was better than sex: 'Both are very hard to stay without and I'm sure sex wouldn't be so rewarding as this World Cup. It's not that sex isn't good but the World Cup is every four years and sex is not.' The ever-competitive Roy Keane stated in 2008 that scoring goals was 'the best feeling in the world', not only better than sex but also 'better than drinking'. Controversial stuff. Paul Ince espoused the even less convincing view that tackling was better than sex.

Former Chelsea striker Jimmy Floyd Hasselbaink saw the whole thing from a different point of view, being of the opinion that those who thought scoring a goal was better than sex were 'not having proper sex'. Julie Burchill was also with the doubters on this one. In 1998, she wrote in *The Guardian*: 'It has become, in recent years, cool to say that you find football more exciting than sex . . . Frankly, any man who prefers football to sex is going to be one of the lousiest lays this side of Andy Capp.'

PETER THE GREAT

The impact of a high-profile career in football on a man's sex life was best captured by Peter Crouch. When asked, 'What would you be if you weren't a footballer?' he replied, with a degree of modesty not often found in a top player, 'Probably a virgin!'

THE LOVE TRIANGLE

Footballers have given a whole new meaning to the phrase 'playing away' through their marital infidelities. Although 'Cashley' and Cheryl Cole and Posh and Becks became tabloid targets because of accusations of extramarital liaisons, few affairs have caught the public imagination to the same degree as the one between Sven-Göran Eriksson, who was in a relationship with Italian-American lawyer Nancy Dell'Olio, and former weathergirl Ulrika Jonsson in 2002. Of course, Sven also earned infamy as part of another love triangle when in 2004 it emerged that he had had an affair with FA secretary Faria Alam. The FA's chief executive Mark Palios, who had also been involved with Alam, resigned in the wake of the scandal.

The Sven-Ulrika-Nancy 'romance' did create some comedy moments. A *Sunday Mirror* cartoon depicted Sven telling Ulrika, 'Never mind Beckham's toe, let's play footsie.' The Irish football sketch show *Après Match* had a particularly amusing take on the love triangle, using the revelations to poke fun at Sven's bland answers in press interviews:

INTERVIEWER: 'Sven, how do you feel about the World Cup?'
SVEN: 'I'm feeling very optimistic.'
INTERVIEWER: 'How would you feel if you found Ulrika Jonsson naked in your bed?'
SVEN: 'I'd be very optimistic.'

The whole thing became a major talking point. On his radio show *The Last Word*, Eamon Dunphy dealt with the episode in the context of the media's intrusion into the private lives of public figures. The following exchange took a turn for the impartial, though:

EAMON DUNPHY: 'We wouldn't have published it [the Sven–Ulrika story] here.'
ROY GREENSLADE: 'You would if Mick McCarthy had been having an affair with Andrea Corr.'
EAMON DUNPHY: 'That would've been regarded as a bloody miracle. Have you seen Mick McCarthy?'

Sven himself would later remark, 'It's no good lying in bed at night wondering if you've made the right choice.' No, he wasn't deliberating over Ulrika or Nancy – just his choice of pieces for his classical compilation CD, *The Sven-Göran Eriksson Classical Collection*.

A MOTHER'S LOVE

One woman who has always been loyal to Sven is his mother. When she was asked about the affair with Ulrika she reportedly remarked: 'When he rings me, he always talks to me about the weather but never about the weathergirl.'

POSITION VACANT

Not long after Sven's affair with Faria Alam is revealed, the CIA advertise an opening for an assassin. After all of the background checks, interviews and tests are done, there are three finalists, two men and one woman. For the final test, an agent takes the first candidate to a large metal door and hands him a gun.

'We must know that you will follow your instructions, no matter what the circumstances. Inside this room, you will find your wife sitting on a chair. You have to kill her.'

The man says, 'You can't be serious. I could never shoot my wife.'

The agent replies, 'Then you're not the right man for the job.'

The second man is given the same instructions. He takes the gun and goes into the room. All is quiet for about five minutes. Then the agent comes out with tears in his eyes and says, 'I tried, but I can't kill my wife.'

The agent tells him, 'You don't have what it takes. Get your wife and go home.'

Finally, it's Nancy's turn and she is told she must kill Sven. She takes the gun into the room. Shots are heard. Then there's screaming, crashing, banging on the walls. After a few minutes, all is quiet again. The door opens slowly and there stands Nancy, sweat dripping from her brow. She says, 'You didn't tell me the gun was loaded with blanks. I beat him to death with the chair.'

ANYTHING GOES

Sven's eye for the ladies was memorably celebrated by Manchester City fans during his time as their manager. To the tune of 'Lord of the Dance' they chanted:

> Sven, Sven, wherever you may be
> You are the pride of Man City
> You can shag my wife on our settee
> If we win the cup at Wemb-er-ley.

It seems, in fact, that Sven will never be allowed to forget his reputation as a ladies' man. When it was announced that he was to take up the position of director of football with Second Division Notts County, the *Daily Mirror* featured a cartoon that had Sven asking: 'So is it true that there are five women for every man in Nottingham?' Others asked, in the spirit of Mrs Merton, 'Tell me, Sven, what was it that attracted you to the billionaire bankers of Notts County?'

STAN THE MAN

'Svengate' was not Ulrika's first involvement with football. One of her ex-boyfriends was Stan Collymore. In 2004, Collymore was revealed to have participated in 'dogging', which entails hanging around in car parks having sex with strangers. In his autobiography, Collymore became football's most famous kiss-and-tell artist when he listed a number of women with whom he had had intimate relations, including fellow celebrities Davina McCall, Sara Cox and Kirsty Gallacher. When the book emerged, Liverpool fans wistfully remarked that it was a pity he had not scored as frequently at Anfield.

Loyalty wasn't always one of Collymore's strengths as a player, either, as the following confusing comment reveals: 'I faxed a transfer request to the club at the beginning of the week, but let me state that I don't want to leave Leicester.'

WHAT WOMEN WANT

A woman who had been dating Stan Collymore was walking along the beach, when she found a bottle in the sand. When she picked it up a genie appeared in front of her. 'I'll grant you three wishes for freeing me, but beware, as whatever you wish for, your ex-love will get twice as much.'

'But that rat left me for another,' replied the woman.

'I'm sorry, but that's what it says in the rule book,' said the genie.

'All right. First, I want a million pounds.' A great heap of cash appeared at her feet, and far away a pile twice as big materialised at Stan's feet.

'Second, I want a diamond necklace.' A beautiful necklace appeared, and Stan suddenly found himself with two.

'And third,' she said, 'please scare me half to death.'

UNRESOLVED QUESTIONS

Not long after the story of Ashley Cole's infidelity broke, Chelsea visited Rome, and Ashley took the opportunity to meet the Pope.

Instead of just an hour, as scheduled, the meeting goes on for two days. Finally, a weary Cole emerges to face the waiting news media. Though tired, Cole is smiling and announces that the summit has been a resounding success. He says he and the Pope agreed on 80 per cent of the matters they discussed, and then he heads off to rejoin the rest of the squad.

A few minutes later, the Pope comes out to make his statement. He looks tired, discouraged and close to tears. Sadly, he announces that his meeting with Cole has been a failure.

Incredulous, one reporter asks, 'But Your Holiness, Mr Cole just told us that the summit was a great success and you agreed on 80 per cent of what you discussed.'

Exasperated, the Pope answers, 'Yes, but we were talking about the ten commandments.'

UP TO HIS NECK IN IT

At Christmas, Cheryl Cole goes to the men's section of a department store to buy a white dress shirt for her husband. When the shop assistant asks about his collar size, Mrs Cole looks unsure at first, but then her face brightens. She holds up her hands, forming a circle with her forefingers and thumbs. 'I don't know his size,' she says, 'but my hands fit perfectly around his neck.'

ABSENCE MAKES THE HEART GROW FONDER

In a way, it's no wonder that professional footballers seem to struggle so much. They often have to be away from home and it can hardly be conducive to domestic bliss. But as Rafa Benitez realises, it could be worse. They could be cricketers. The Liverpool manager pondered the question, 'How can you tell your wife you are just popping out to play a match and then not come back for five days?'

OOH, MATRON!

Birmingham City director Karren Brady once commented, 'Footballers are only interested in drinking, clothes and the size of their willies.' Maybe it's the proximity of all that testosterone, but sex seems to find its way into football commentary whether the pundits like it or not.

'Brazil – they're so good it's like they are running around the pitch playing with themselves.'

John Motson

'Phil Neville. Today he's at full-back. In the last game he took over the Butt holding role.'

BBC Radio 5 Live commentator

'The crowd gave the players an arousing reception.'

Packie Bonner

'There are the boys, their balls between their legs.'

Amanda Reddington, GMTV

'Marian Pahars is imminent. He's stripped off and ready to come.'

Clive Tyldesley

'For me, the book is still open on Totti.'

Ron Atkinson

'The Brazil coach says it's the standing up, jiggy stuff that causes problems but if they lay down and do it slowly, that's all right.'

Gabby Logan during the 2002 World Cup

'I don't like to see players tossed off needlessly.'

Andy Gray complaining about an overzealous referee

'The Europeans just have to feel you and they will go down.'

Denis Irwin

'Every time Zidane comes inside, Roberto Carlos just goes bonking down the wing.'

Ron Atkinson

PUNINTENTIONAL

Naturally enough, commentators in other sports sometimes have trouble with these issues, too. Cricket seems to be particularly fruitful. Brian Johnston, who collapsed into giggles on air when his fellow commentator Jonathan Agnew noted that Ian Botham 'just couldn't quite get his leg over', came out with the all-time classic of the genre when he made the perfectly accurate remark, 'The bowler's Holding, the batsman's Willey.'

Snooker commentator Ted Lowe famously remarked, 'Fred Davis, the doyen of snooker, now 67 years of age and too old to get his leg over, prefers to use his left hand.'

In athletics, meanwhile, it seems romance dies with marriage. David Coleman observed, 'And there is no "I love you" message because Steve Ovett has married the girl.'

SEX, FANS AND VIDEOTAPE

In his autobiography, former Gunners midfielder Emmanuel Petit recalled regular meetings with a pretty girl at a hotel near Arsenal's training ground. On one occasion, he wrote, they had sex in the snooker room. The following morning, the hotel director and the staff greeted him with applause. He was informed that the room was fitted with security cameras and they had seen everything. Happily for Petit, they were all Arsenal fans and the footage went no further.

EVERLASTING LOVE

When it comes to prioritising football and love, fans rarely have any problems recognising which is the more important, as the following story illustrates.

Two Manchester United fans were on their way to Old Trafford when a funeral cortège passed. One of the men stopped, took his cap off and bowed his head. The other followed his friend's lead, and after the hearse had passed, he said, 'That was very respectful of you.'

The other man replied, 'Well, it's the least I could do. I was married to her for 50 years.'

STRANGE CHOICE

It may sometimes seem as if footballers are only interested in busty blondes and sultry brunettes, but it's not always all about the glamour. When asked in a Leeds United programme questionnaire which film star he would like to be washed up on a desert island with, Darren Huckerby replied, 'Robert De Niro.'

Reading's Graeme Murty responded to the same question with, 'Joan of Arc – the one who rode naked through the streets.'

WHAT'S LOVE GOT TO DO WITH IT?

Soccer may be the beautiful game, but it can ruin a beautiful thing. Joanne Bradley from Kent divorced her husband Neil on the grounds that he was obsessed with Norwich City. Things started to go wrong when he painted their bedroom yellow and green while she was out. Things deteriorated when he took her on a romantic holiday. At first glance this might seem like a good idea, but the problem was that his idea of a romantic holiday was to take her to Norwich to watch the team training. The final straw came when he bought her an anniversary present – a pair of Norwich City knickers. She commented, 'When he came back with the knickers, I went mad. He seemed to think they were sexy!'

THE FINAL WORD

Women often suffer at the hands of sports-mad husbands. Elsie Revie, wife of the legendary Don, manager of Leeds United, would say to her two children, 'See that man walking past the window? That man's your father.'

Some men are fortunate enough to have spouses who tolerate their sporting obsessions. Bill Shankly famously quashed rumours about an anniversary treat for his wife, saying, 'Of course I didn't take my wife to see Rochdale as an anniversary present. It was her birthday. Would I have got married during the football season? And, anyway, it wasn't Rochdale, it was Rochdale reserves.'

Before setting off for the Charity Shield one season, Shanks is reputed to have asked his wife, 'Do you have anything to say before the football season starts?'

His wife must have been delighted to hear him say: 'I was the best manager in Britain because I was never devious or cheated anyone. I'd break my wife's legs if I played against her, but I'd never cheat her.'

A MAN'S WORLD

Footballers' wives might have a lot to put up with at times, but it's nothing compared with the flak that's sometimes come the way of female players. It might not be surprising to find Brian Clough saying, 'I like my women to be feminine, not sliding into tackles and covered in mud,' but it was another matter when FIFA president Sepp Blatter suggested in 2004 that women should play in skimpier kit to 'create a more female aesthetic'. 'Let the women play in more feminine clothes like they do in volleyball,' said the most senior man in the game. 'They could, for example, have tighter shorts.'

In 1997, Maureen McGonigle, head of women's football in Scotland, made an irrefutable point about the criteria on which female players are judged, saying, 'If football in the Premier Division on any given Saturday was going to be restricted to good-looking [male] players, there wouldn't be many matches going on.'

DO YOU THINK I'M SEXY?

Musings on aspects of love and sex have provided some classic football quotes over the seasons, as the following compendium documents.

'For some men at least, in the match between football and sex, football will always scrape home on goal difference.'

Joe O'Connor

'Even though there is no question that sex is a nicer activity than watching football (no nil–nil draws, no offside trap, no cup upsets, *and* you're warm), in the normal run of things, the feelings it engenders are simply not as intense as those brought about by a once-in-a-lifetime last-minute Championship winner.'

Nick Hornby, Fever Pitch

'I like him because he's got such a nice arse.'

Mrs Emmanuel Petit opts for a bum deal

'If you want, as a footballer, you can always have sex.'

Juan Sebastián Verón rubs it in

'His brains are between his legs. That is what has caused his downfall. He thinks it is fine to parade all over the place with females of dubious reputation.'

Trinidad and Tobago FA chief Jack Warner, sounding just a wee bit censorious about Dwight Yorke

'I'm a footballer, not a tart.'

Michael Owen reminds us why he's football's Mr Clean

'We interrupt this marriage to bring you the football season.'

Slogan on a mug owned by Kenny Dalglish and his wife Marina

'When I first heard about Viagra, I thought it was a new player Chelsea had just signed.'

Former sports minister Tony Banks

'Like sex, the movements in football are limited and predictable.'

Peter Ackroyd

'John Bond has blackened my name with his insinuations about the private lives of football managers. Both my wives are upset.'

Malcolm Allison

'What a silly world. Now we are restraining from making love with someone the day before a game. What a cynical world.'

David Ginola

'Good strikers can only score goals when they have had good sex on the night before a match.'

Brazilian forward Romario

'I'd rather have a guy take me to a football match and have a drink afterwards than go to bed with someone.'

Samantha Fox

'Hump it, bump it, whack it! It might be a recipe for a good sex life, but it won't win the World Cup.'

Ken Bates referring to Graham Taylor's tactics as England manager in 1993

'If Rod Stewart can't pull the best-looking girls in the world, what chance do the rest of us have?'

Mo Johnston ruefully reflects that fame can't always buy you love

'Last season I was sent off in two successive games and my wife Louise dropped me from her Fantasy League team.'

Dion Dublin

'I got so many kisses after this goal that they would have sufficed a modest woman for a lifetime.'

Ferenc Puskás on scoring for Hungary in the 1952 Olympic final

'To suggest a player shouldn't have sex the night before a match is the height of silliness. I've had enjoyable nights and mornings before a game and it never affected me. But before a match I won't put a lot of energy into it.'

Graeme Souness

'The orgies, the birds and the fabulous money. Football is just a distraction.'

Peter Storey, ex-Arsenal star

'It's not the sex that tires out young footballers, it's staying up half the night looking for it.'

Clemens Westerhof, Nigeria coach at USA '94

'It's tight, taut and muscular. Bobby Moore's posterior comes top of our Girls' Bottom League.'

John Samuel

'Runners-up at Wembley four times. Never the bride, always the bridegrooms, Leicester City.'

Peter Jones

'You can compare us at the moment to a bit of soft porn – there's an awful lot of foreplay and not a lot going on in the box.'

Rochdale manager Keith Hill after a home defeat

'The playboy of United, Dwight Yorke, came on in the second half and showed the crowd that he could do equally well on the pitch what he usually does in the Dublin nightclubs: scoring from close range.'

Mick Clifford in the Sunday Tribune

'A man so dull he once made the papers for having a one-in-the-bed romp.'

Comedian Nick Hancock on Alan Shearer

ONE MOMENT IN TIME

Chris Waddle once admitted: 'If we go out on a Saturday night, I'm back in time for *Match of the Day*. If we ever get divorced, the missus will be naming Sky as the other party.'

The anecdotal evidence suggests that Mrs Waddle is not alone. One football widow was having a go at her husband. 'Your whole life is football,' she moaned. 'You never take me out, you never buy me presents. You're either at the match or watching football on the telly. I bet you can't even remember when our wedding anniversary is!'

'Of course I can,' replied the husband. 'It's the same date that Michael Owen scored his first hat-trick.'

AMONGST WOMEN

Extensive work has been done on researching the question 'If England's best-known football teams were women, who would they be?' The following are the findings of the study:

Arsenal – Angelina Jolie
Always look good, maverick at times, but sometimes they really feel the Pitts.

Aston Villa – Dido
One big hit. A bit bland.

Blackburn Rovers – Dot Cotton from *EastEnders*
Common as muck, constantly worrying.

Chelsea – Kate in *Lost*
Every bit looks good from all angles. But what are they doing with him?

Fulham – Rachel Stevens
Fine to look at but on the small side.

Leeds United – Sarah Palin
Generally hard to see why people like them.

Luton Town – The Nolan Sisters
Had a brief taste of glory but no longer in the mood for dancing.

Manchester City – Leona Lewis
Rags to riches. Came into a lot of money unexpectedly.

Manchester United – Mariah Carey
Occasionally interesting, frequently annoying.

Middlesbrough – Chrissie Hynde
On the face of it the glory days are over, but you're quite interested to see what they're going to do next.

Newcastle United – Madonna
Great in the past but have now lost the plot a bit.

Spurs – Joan Collins
Used to look good but living on past glories.

West Ham – Britney Spears
Ability to fascinate but not always in the way they might
want.

A RESULT

Ian Holloway gave an unintentionally revealing insight into
modern football culture with his choice of (very extended)
metaphor after his QPR team drew with Chesterfield in
2003: 'To put it in gentleman's terms, if you've been out for
a night and you're looking for a young lady and you pull
one, you've done what you set out to do. We didn't look our
best today, but we've pulled. Some weeks the lady is good
looking and some weeks they're not. Our performance today
would have been not the best-looking bird, but at least we
got her in the taxi. She may not have been the best-looking
lady we ended up taking home, but it was still very pleasant
and very nice, so thanks very much and let's have coffee.'

PARIS-IAN ROMANCE

Although Cristiano Ronaldo smashed the world transfer
record when he moved from Manchester United to Real
Madrid in the summer of 2009, he also made the headlines
that week because he was spotted canoodling with famous-
for-being-famous heiress Paris Hilton, which naturally led to
much sniggering about potential headlines like 'Ronaldo in
Paris' and 'Ronaldo Spends Night in Hilton'. Commenting on
the alliance in the *Sunday Times*, Rod Liddle compared it to
Gordon Brown and Susan Boyle getting together. Presumably
he meant to say that it didn't really bear thinking about.

There are two schools of thought on Ronaldo's sex appeal.
There is his own: 'It would be hypocritical of me to say I think

I'm ugly.' Then there's Derby manager Paul Jewell's view: 'If he was good looking, you'd say he has everything.'

Prospective WAGs should take encouragement from the fact that he is not as shallow as some footballers: 'For me, it is what is inside a beautiful woman that is important. Although she must also be beautiful, like Angelina Jolie.'

13

WHEN IRISH EYES ARE SMILING

———⚽———

'If Ireland had scored more goals, they would have won the match.'

Jimmy Magee

In 1964, FIFA brought in a new rule that allowed footballers to play for a country other than that in which they were born if they were qualified, by ancestry or residence, to claim citizenship of the country in question. Since then, it's sometimes been said that a true Ireland fan is one who knows the nationality of all the players on the squad.

Manchester United's Shay Brennan was the first player to declare for Ireland under the new Football Association of Ireland (FAI) regulation. The Manchester-born full-back played nineteen times for Ireland, captaining the side five times. Brennan was at the heart of a memorable exchange with his Manchester United colleague Bill Foulkes.

SHAY: 'How's the mouth?'
FOULKES [with four stitches in his mouth]: 'She's at home with the kids.'

In 1982, Shay went down to Greystones to watch a rugby match between Greystones and the 1982 Triple Crown-winning side, played to mark the Wicklow team's jubilee season. Rugby legend Moss Keane was down to go to the game too. In Greystones, they are well used to big names

in the rugby world visiting but they are not accustomed to
famous football personalities like Shay.

Mossie was with Brennan in the bar, having consumed a few
drinks. He was a little cheesed off that Shay was getting all the
attention. Everyone was asking Brennan questions, but, very
unusually, Keane was being ignored. Eventually, Moss threw
in a question: 'Who played soccer for Scotland and cricket for
England?' There was total silence. Everyone in the bar was a
sports fan and they were all scratching their heads trying to
figure out this riddle. Finally they were all forced to concede
defeat. Moss walked out as soon as he'd provided the answer:
'Denis Law and Ian Botham!'

SONG FOR IRELAND

Brennan was the first in a long line of players to declare for
Ireland. One of the most infamous of this motley crew was
QPR defender Terry Mancini. According to folklore, on his
Ireland debut against Poland in 1973, as the anthems were
played Mancini turned around to one of his teammates and
said, 'God, the Polish anthem doesn't half go on.' He was
abruptly told, 'Shut up. That's the Irish anthem.'

Fellow Irish international Don Givens scored one goal
for Man United in his nine appearances, four as substitute,
in his short stay with the club. He moved to Luton in 1970
for £15,000 before really establishing his reputation with a
talented QPR side in which he scored 76 goals in 242 games.
Legend has it that Givens was once given a rather unusual
task. His teammate Mancini was having such a run of scoring
own goals that Givens was brought back to mark him every
time QPR conceded a corner!

KEEPING UP WITH THE JONES

Ireland's propensity to attract players through the citizenship
rule led to a rash of jokes such as 'The FAI stands for "Find
An Irishman"' and 'All you need to do to qualify to play for
Ireland is to drink a pint of Guinness.' The jokes reached a

peak when Vinnie Jones, or 'Vinnie O'Jones' as the tabloid press christened him, sought to qualify for Ireland. When he came over to Dublin to check for his grandmother's records the *Daily Star*'s headline was: 'Begorrah! I'm off to pick up my passport now, Jack.'

Vinnie went on to play for Wales. According to one mischievous report, he heard of his call-up in the following way:

MIKE SMITH: 'Hi, Vinnie. I'm the manager of Wales and we'd like you to play for us. You do like Wales, Vinnie?'
JONES: 'Of course I do, I've seen *Moby Dick* twice!'

It is no exaggeration to say that Jimmy Greaves was under-whelmed by the news that Jones had gained international status: 'Well, stone me! We've had cocaine, bribery and Arsenal scoring two goals at home. But just when you thought there truly were no surprises left in football, Vinnie Jones turns out to be an international player.'

CHINESE WHISPERS

Northern Ireland are not as famous for their generous application of the parentage laws as their southern counterparts. In 1980, Everton manager Gordon Lee rang up Billy Bingham to recommend one of his midfielders, Eamon O'Keefe, for the Northern Ireland squad. Lee was shocked to discover that he didn't qualify and indignantly asked, 'Well, what business has anyone got naming him Eamon O'Keefe if he isn't Irish?'

Bingham replied, 'Probably the same business they have naming you Lee when you're not Chinese!'

LITERARY CENTRE CIRCLES

Canadian-born Jimmy Nicholl moved with his family to Belfast in 1957. He joined United as an apprentice straight from school in 1972 and turned professional two years later. Nicholl was capped 73 times for Northern Ireland, culminating in appearances at the World Cup finals in 1982 and 1986.

George Best told a wonderful story about Jimmy Nicholl's involvement with the national team. In 1978, the squad were making their way from their hotel to Windsor Park for a fixture against Iceland. Their manager was Billy Bingham, a very erudite man. Throughout the bus journey, Bingham was enthralled by the book he was reading and oblivious to everything that was going on around him. Eventually, some officials summoned him to the top of the bus. George rushed up to see what he was reading. Nicholl asked what it was.

'*The Diaries of James Joyce, 1930 to 1935*,' George replied.

A few minutes later, Nicholl tapped Best on the shoulder and said, 'This Joyce must have been some kid. He kept a diary up to when he was a five-year-old child?'

KEANE BY NAME, KEEN BY NATURE

For most of his teenage years, Roy Keane was told he was too small to make it as a footballer, an error of judgement comparable to that made by the man at Decca who turned the Beatles down, telling Brian Epstein that 'guitar groups are on the way out'.

When he was 17, Keane got a part-time contract with League of Ireland club Cobh Ramblers. Part of the package was a football course in Dublin. A year later, he was signed by Nottingham Forest, a snip at £25,000. Brian Clough said of his young protégé, 'I couldn't understand a word he was saying. But his feet told me all I wanted to know.'

As a player with Manchester United and as manager of Sunderland, Keane, now in charge of Ipswich Town, has never been known to mince his words, as the following exchange illustrates.

REPORTER: 'Have you ever thought of a career in the media?'

ROY KEANE: 'No, no. I want a proper job.'

Keane also has a talent for damning with faint praise, as former teammates at Manchester United are all too aware. He was prone to making observations like, 'It was an excellent cross by Gary [Neville]. I was surprised by the quality of it.'

Keane showed his acid tongue when he mused on Sunderland's efforts to get Kenwyne Jones back from the Caribbean: 'We have to help with the travel arrangements. If we let them [the Trinidad and Tobago FA], I think he'd be on a ferry.'

No, there's no messing when Keane's around, and he doesn't miss a trick, either, as his comment on signing Andy Reid for Sunderland proves: 'He's not six foot four. I don't think he ever will be.'

I, KEANO

Keane triggered Ireland's second civil war when his verbal attack on manager Mick McCarthy during the 2002 World Cup saw Ireland's greatest player flying home from the tournament even before a ball was kicked. There was no grey area. Irish fans were either for McCarthy or for Keane. The saga spawned a phenomenally successful musical, *I, Keano*, and several good lines.

'I wouldn't send a player home, but if I did, he would probably be the best player in the world.'

Keane fans' adaptation of the Carlsberg ad

'Michael Collins and Roy Keane. Two heroic Corkmen both shot in the back.'

T-shirt slogan spotted in Cork

'Sometimes, I think he thinks he's Alex Ferguson.'

Jason McAteer on Keane

'One pair of hardly used Diadora football boots: contact Roy Keane. Reason for sale: just got too big for them.'

Ad in the Hull Daily Mail *after the bust-up*

'Oh, I'd have sent him home, all right, but I'd have shot him first.'

Brian Clough comes down on McCarthy's side

'Sending that twat home.'

Mick McCarthy, when asked at a Sunderland fans' event in 2003 what was the highlight of his time as Ireland manager

THE PURSUIT OF EXCELLENCE

A friend of mine was telling me that he sent his son to the Roy Keane school of excellence. The boy came back effing and blinding, wouldn't sit in the back of the car and refused to share a room!

BIG MAC

As a player, Mick McCarthy was not known for his pace or his first touch. To his credit, he is the first to recognise this himself. During the year of his greatest triumph, when he captained Ireland to the World Cup finals in 1990, he said, 'The only thing is, I'm not quick. We all know that. I mean, I go out running and a woman with a pram passes me.'

He was always a man to wear his heart on his sleeve: 'My heart was pounding and I was feeling as sick as the proverbial donkey.' Even when he tried to keep his cards close to his chest, it didn't quite work out: 'I could come in after a game like that [Ireland v. Andorra] and say that it was awful, it was bobbins, we didn't play well, we didn't get great crosses in, we could have scored more goals, we were pure shit. I could say that, but I'm not going to.' However, he is not a believer in verbosity: 'Anyone who uses the word "quintessentially" in a half-time talk is talking crap.'

After McCarthy resigned, Ireland played Greece in a friendly with Don Givens acting as caretaker manager. Asked about Ireland's prospects, Gary Doherty replied, 'It's a no-win game for us, although I suppose we can win by winning.' During his time at Spurs, the Tottenham fans, with their tongues firmly in their cheeks, christened Doherty 'Ginger Pelé'.

THE LIFE OF BRIAN

McCarthy's successor as Ireland manager was Brian Kerr. He's one of the nice guys of the sport, but he's not above pulling a stunt to confuse the opposition. During his days as manager of St Pat's, when he heard that representatives from Dinamo Bucharest were watching a training session in advance of a European tie, to ensure the opposition were as bemused as possible he instructed his side to play a Gaelic football match for the entire session!

A PICTURE IS WORTH A THOUSAND WORDS

Pride comes before a fall. In 1990, Andy Townsend was walking with his wife in Dublin. It was shortly after the World Cup and everywhere they went people were asking for Andy's autograph and requesting to have their photo taken with him. Eventually, they decided to head for a quieter part of the capital.

They were walking along when Andy noticed a woman brandishing a camera. Instinctively, he stopped and posed for a picture. After a pregnant pause, the woman yelled, 'You stupid eejit! Will you get out of the f***ing way!' Andy turned around to see a beautiful statue behind him.

THE BLARNEY STONE

One of Ireland's biggest tourist attractions is the Blarney Stone, which supposedly endows visitors who kiss it with 'the gift of the gab'. This may be a mixed blessing, as Ireland's commentators, players, managers and administrators have produced as much nonsense as insight.

'It's 110 degrees and it has to be said that it's well over 100.'

George Hamilton, RTÉ

'And there's a free kick now in the box, just in that little space between the eighteen-yard line and the six-yard line, that little incomplete rectangle. I don't know what you'd call that geometrically, that three-sided rectangle.'

Today FM's Tom Tyrell

'And Celtic have extended their lead at the top to a remarkable 15 points. Now to soccer . . .'

TV3 frontman Trevor Welch

'The Baggio brothers, of course, are not related.'

Which is it, George Hamilton?

'If we had taken our chances we would have won – at least.'

David O'Leary on another Aston Villa disappointment

'If the fourth official had done his job correctly, it wouldn't have happened . . . but I don't want to blame anyone.'

Tranmere boss John Aldridge

'Most of the play is in the middle of the pitch, like a giant Easter egg.'

Tom Tyrell

'Achilles tendon injuries are the worst you can probably have – they're a pain in the butt.'

David O'Leary

'Certain allegations have been made against me and I know who the alligators are.'

Former FAI official

'Are you Tim Henman in disguise?'

> *Bohemians fans to Shamrock Rovers*
> *after the Hoops led 4–1 but lost 6–4*

'We are about as far away from the penalty box as the penalty box is from us.'

> *Tom Tyrell*

'I was a young lad when I was growing up.'

> *David O'Leary*

'Gary Breen ruled out for Republic because of a groin stain.'

> *Curious caption on* Sky News

'I've no problems with our defence, even with Ian Harte at left-back.'

> *Ray Houghton*

'Jesus, I only wanted you to pass the salt.'

> *Roy Keane, having been on the receiving end of a heartfelt*
> *monologue by Tony Adams at a UEFA dinner in 2003*

'Roy Keane would never let his emotions destabilise the team.'

> *Niall Quinn's crystal ball was on the blink in 1999*

'A win is a win, if you win it.'

> *Ireland manager Steve Staunton, after a draw*

LAST TRAIN TO MUNICH

Drink features prominently in the lore of Irish football. Cork City famously came up against giants Bayern Munich in a UEFA Cup tie in 1991. Cork's manager Noel O'Mahony didn't sound too perturbed when asked if he was afraid of losing the away leg: 'We'd still be happy if we lose. It's on at the same time as the beer festival.'

CHEAP GIFT

Following an ongoing saga of cock-ups and administrative
failures, Irish fans tend to be very critical of the FAI, as the
following conversation reveals.

FATHER: 'Son, what'll I buy you for your birthday?'
SON: 'A bicycle!'
FATHER: 'What'll I buy you for your first communion?'
SON: 'A PlayStation!'
FATHER: 'What'll I buy you for Christmas?'
SON: 'A Mickey Mouse outfit!'
FATHER: 'No problem, son. I'll get you the FAI.'

DENIS THE MENACE

Cork native Denis Irwin won 56 caps and was one of Alex
Ferguson's best buys at Man United. At Irwin's testimonial
dinner, Jack Charlton brought the house down with his
unconventional tribute to Denis. Jack said, 'Denis was the
consummate professional; the best full-back to play for
Manchester United, the best full-back to play for the Republic
of Ireland. He was always our most consistent player: he never
made mistakes; he never gave the ball away; he was always
on time for training, always first on the bus for training. He
never let you down nor once caused a problem. What a boring
f***ing bastard!'

In 2008, Denis attended a press event in Manchester and was
asked by a young journalist, 'Denis, do you remember where
you were when United won the Treble in Barcelona in 1999?'

Irwin coolly replied, 'Oh, yes, son. I was playing left-back.'

TERRIFICALLY TALENTED THREESOME

After Ireland beat Italy in the 1994 World Cup finals in
the United States, the lead singer of Ireland's most famous
group, U2, was challenged by a TV interviewer to name three
members of Ireland's football team. Bono answered, 'Joyce,
Synge and Beckett.'

THE HAIRDRYER TREATMENT

Different managers have different styles. Some favour a fire-and-brimstone approach. During his spell at Birmingham City, the former Shelbourne star striker Eric Barber was twelfth man for a league match at a time when no substitutes were used during play. The twelfth man was only used if there was an injury or illness.

Birmingham were slaughtered in the match but that indignity was as nothing compared with the humiliation each player was subjected to by their manager. He started off with the goalkeeper and went one by one through the other ten players – pointing out very emphatically and in great detail just how ineffectual each of them was. Eric was fervently thanking God that he had not been selected, because he would escape the tongue-lashing. He was wrong. After the manager had finished with the team, he turned to Barber and said, 'And as for you, you're not even good enough to play for this shower of useless no-hopers.'

GILESY

One manager not in that tradition is John Giles. The Leeds legend is credited with finally dragging the Republic of Ireland into the professional era during his tenure as manager. He was blessed with Irish diplomacy, i.e. the ability to tell a man to go to hell in such a way that he actually looks forward to the trip.

In conversation with this scribe, Ray Treacy spoke of his great respect for his former boss, but admitted that he had regularly exploited Giles' one weakness. He couldn't say the words 'specific' or 'specifically'. Instead, he said 'pacific' or 'pacifically'. When he gave his team talks, he would always get it wrong and Treacy would start pretending to row a boat and sing, 'Row, row, row the boat, gently down the stream.' It always made Giles go red in the face and bark at Ray to shut up.

In 1977, to the astonishment of many, Giles turned his back on life as a player-manager with First Division West Bromwich Albion in favour of League of Ireland football with Shamrock Rovers. It was a big adjustment for him. His last game in England was a local derby match against Aston Villa, played in front of 52,000 at Villa Park. Then his next competitive game was against Thurles Town in front of 92 at the Greyhound Stadium. That must have been disappointing for Giles, who once said, 'I'd rather play in front of a full house than an empty crowd.'

A BUN FIGHT

Sports administration can get very political. In 1980, Giles resigned as Ireland boss and a 16-man committee of the FAI was chosen to decide who would be the next manager. They were to deliberate on the respective merits of Eoin Hand and Paddy Mulligan. In the vote, Hand emerged victorious by nine to seven. One of the committee members was reported to have said that the only reason he voted for Hand was that he suspected Mulligan of being the person who had thrown a bun at him on one of the foreign trips!

WORDS OF WISDOM

Following his retirement from management, Giles became a media pundit, a task that he enjoys, although perhaps his expectations weren't very high: 'Analysis is not nearly as stressful as management. I haven't been shot yet!'

Not for Gilesy the type of statements associated with some of his fellow former internationals, like Frank Stapleton ('You've got to be careful. You're not sure if the ball is going to bounce up or down.'), Andy Townsend ('Scotland can't afford to take their minds off the gas.') and David O'Leary: 'The surprise for me, and I'm delighted for Gary Kelly, but Steve Finnan, for me, has had an outstanding season for Fulham, but, as I say, that's the only surprise, even though, as I say, I'm delighted for Gary.'

THE ODD COUPLE

Giles feels that his partnership with Eamon Dunphy on RTÉ works because of the contrast in personalities. 'Love him or loathe him,' he says of Keano's biggest fan, 'you can't ignore him.'

Their partnership, and Bill O'Herlihy's chairmanship, was memorably celebrated by the late, great Dermot Morgan, star of *Father Ted*, in the much missed *Scrap Saturday* series. In one memorable sketch, O'Herlihy broke the news that Dunphy was to have a child by Giles. Consternation ensued, though, when it emerged that Bono rather than Giles had fathered Dunphy's baby.

Eamon Dunphy joined Manchester United as an apprentice in 1960, at the age of 15. After two years at Old Trafford, he signed professional forms, but he never made it onto the first team. Capped 23 times for Ireland, he jokes, 'I won most of them because John Giles didn't turn up.'

In the late 1960s, Dunphy was one of the leaders in the campaign to get an Ireland manager who would be allowed to pick the team. Previously, the side had been chosen by a selection committee, with disastrous results. After helping to achieve this democratic revolution when Mick Meagan was appointed manager, Eamo was chosen for Meagan's first game in charge against Austria at Dalymount. Dunphy jokes that he asked Mick to substitute him at half-time because he'd been exhausted by the campaign and frankly he was an embarrassment to democracy.

In 2002, when speculation was rife as to who would replace Mick McCarthy, Eamon Dunphy was asked if he'd like the job. He replied, 'I'd love to do it, but I couldn't afford the wage cut.'

A whole book would be needed to feature all of Eamo's stories and comments, but the following are worthy of special mention:

'Kilbane's head is better than his feet. If only he had three heads, one on the end of each leg.'

'Ha, ha, ha, that's the first time I've seen sex between two men on the BBC.'

On a cosy interview between
Garth Crooks and Sven-Göran Eriksson

'If Rio Ferdinand is worth £100,000 a week, then this guy is worth 100 million euros . . . a day.'

On Fabio Cannavaro

'After watching Watford against Manchester City last night, that was like a bubble bath. It was beautiful.'

On a Barcelona match

'I will be supporting Germany and Saudi Arabia in the contests ahead.'

On the 2002 World Cup

'You need poverty and dictatorship to produce great footballers.'

'Eamon Dunphy is a nobody with one virtue: honesty and realism.'

A TONY A-WARD

Irish rugby legend Tony Ward also had a distinguished career in the round-ball game. He won an FAI Cup medal with Limerick and played against Kevin Keegan's Southampton in the UEFA Cup. In 1979, he appeared on *A Question of Sport*. He was on Emlyn Hughes' team and Liam Brady was on Gareth Edwards' side. Ward was to witness Colemanspeak at first hand when host David Coleman asked Brady, 'In what sport is a kamen used?' Brady was stumped and very surprised to discover that the answer was hurling. Coleman had completely mispronounced 'camán'.

RED ZONE

One of Ireland's best-known comedians, Mario Rosenstock, is famous for his 'Gift Grub' sketches on Today FM. One of his favourite targets for impersonation is Boyzone singer Ronan Keating. He features Ronan boasting about his credentials as a Manchester United fan and his close friendship with two of their stars 'Mickey Rooney and Franz Ferdinand'.

COLD TURKEY

RTÉ's counterweight to Des 'Anyone but United' Cahill is Ireland's favourite bird, builder, aspiring politician, pop star, Eurovision Song Contest representative, television personality and national institution, Dustin the Turkey. Dustin nailed his red-coloured feathers firmly to the mast when asked for a prediction about a forthcoming clash between United and Liverpool: 'I think it will be a close match so the score will be United 12, Liverpool 0!'

THE MEMORY MAN

Ireland's answer to Motty, Jimmy Magee, has provided Irish football fans with many hours of entertainment, not least when he said, 'Ardiles is stroking the ball as if it was part of his anatomy.' During one Ireland–USSR soccer match when a Russian striker missed an open goal, Jimmy told the viewers at home, 'It's the saltmines for him!' It was also Jimmy who, commentating on an Olympic Games opening ceremony, exclaimed, 'And there it is, the international symbol of peace – the pigeon!'

One of Jimmy's most embarrassing moments came when he was presenting *Junior Sport Magazine* on RTÉ radio in the 1960s. While commentating on sprinting, he momentarily lost the phrase he was searching for as he sought to describe an official hammering down the starting block. Jimmy said, 'And he's taking out his tool now.' With radio listeners trying to get that image out of their heads, he compounded the situation by adding, 'To hammer down his block, of course.'

Jimmy was the face of the popular *Superstars*, which ran on RTÉ in the late '70s. At one stage, he journeyed to the international *Superstars* competition in Tel Aviv. The BBC were also there in force, and Jimmy watched their presenter combing his hair and brushing his impeccable clothes before introducing the programme. The professional image was somewhat undermined by his opening words: 'Here we are in the Holy Land of Israel, a Mecca for tourists.'

RIGHT-HAND MAN

One of Big Jack Charlton's first decisions as Ireland manager was to appoint Maurice Setters as his assistant. Asked to explain the reason, Charlton reportedly replied, 'Maurice is ideal for the job, living as he does in Doncaster.'

14

GAZZA

*'I've never made any predictions about
anything and I never will.'*

Paul Gascoigne

In the last 30 years, no footballer has been taken to people's hearts in the same way as Paul Gascoigne. He may have been described as 'George Best without brains', but we all love a flawed hero, and as the extent of his health problems has emerged, public sympathy for him has grown even greater.

Gascoigne first became something of a national icon when he cried after being booked in the World Cup semi-final in 1990 against West Germany. Really, he should have saved his tears for the Chris Waddle school of penalty taking. The ball Waddle sent over the bar is probably still in outer space.

OLD BONES

In one of his first matches for Newcastle, Gazza was faced with West Ham veteran Billy Bonds. Early in the match, Gazza made a robust tackle on the ageing star. Bonds had a reputation for being a hard man and kids like Gazza did not usually mix it with him.

'Are you all right, Billy?' Gazza asked cheekily.

'It's my ankle,' replied Bonds.

'Oh, that's OK, then. I thought it might be arthritis!'

Bonds had the last laugh by ensuring that Gazza didn't get a kick of the ball after that, though he did give him plenty of kicks.

INTERNATIONAL AFFAIRS

Like many a player, Gazza sometimes struggled with foreign place names. A case in point was when he was selected to play for England B against Iceland in Reykjavik. The young player once described by Bobby Robson as 'the original Milky Bar Kid' and 'a real Billy Bunter' asked plaintively, 'How can I play in a place I can't even say?'

In his autobiography, John Barnes relates that when Sir Bobby was England manager, he walked into a hotel room one day to find him, Chris Waddle and Paul Gascoigne hanging out of the window. Their room was 20 floors up.

'What are you doing?' asked Robson.

Gazza replied, 'I'm throwing soap at these chickens.'

'You're doing what?'

'I'm throwing soap at these chickens,' Gazza repeated.

'Can you really hit them from here?'

'Yeah, of course.'

'Show me.'

Gazza took aim with a piece of soap and scored a direct hit on a chicken. Robson just walked out of the room shaking his head.

A CLOSE SHAVE

After establishing himself as an England international, Gazza was offered a lucrative contract to advertise the aftershave Brut on television. It was a high-profile endorsement that generated a lot of publicity for both parties. On the other hand, there was the potential for disaster.

Gazza was eventually asked the obvious question: 'How long have you been using Brut, Paul?'

'I don't.'

'What aftershave do you use?'
'None. They bring me out in a rash.'

BE PREPARED

In 1996, shortly before the European Championships, Gazza was part of the England squad that caused £5,000 worth of damage on a flight back from a boozy pre-tournament trip to Hong Kong. Maybe they were thinking that even if they showed zero flair on the field of play, at least they'd have proved themselves an attacking force on the plane.

A GUM DEAL

In October 2002, Gazza was to be interviewed for the vacant manager's job at Exeter, but he lost out after the meeting was cancelled at the last minute because he had to have a wisdom tooth removed. It was surely the first time the tabloids had featured the words 'Gazza' and 'wisdom' in the same sentence.

ONE IN A MILLION

Unsurprisingly, given that he's one of the biggest characters in the game, Gazza has inspired some memorable quotes.

'Even at school he was off his head, completely crackers. He'd put his sweets down his socks and then give them to the teachers to eat.'

Steve Stone, fellow England international
who went to school with Gazza

'Comparing Gascoigne to Pelé is like comparing Rolf Harris to Rembrandt.'

Rodney Marsh

'He's a fantastic player when he isn't drunk.'

Brian Laudrup

'Gazza reminds me of Marilyn Monroe. She wasn't the greatest actress in the world, but she was a star, so you didn't mind if she was late.'

Actor Michael Caine

'He's a disgrace . . . thirty going on six.'

Tommy Docherty

'When God gave him this enormous footballing talent, he took his brain out at the same time to equal it up.'

Tony Banks

NOT-SO-FAST FOOD

When Gazza moved to Rangers, he was already a superstar and the Gers fans really took him to their hearts. This was before kebabs, cigarettes and nights on the town with Danny Baker and Chris Evans saw his star in rapid decline. Mind you, Gazza's fitness regime may already have been a bit lacking in Glasgow, city of the deep-fried pizza. Recalling his dietary habits, he said: 'I can't see how one kebab can be the difference between beating one or three men or running from box to box or scoring a goal . . . Bloody hell, in Scotland I had haggis and won the Double!'

SLIM PICKINGS

Having eaten a few too many haggises, Gazza goes to his doctor, who suggests that his health might be better nurtured if he lost a few pounds. The doctor says, 'This is the regime you must follow. Three lettuce leaves, a slice of dry toast and a glass of orange juice twice a day.'

Gazza replies, 'Right. Now is that before meals or after?'

A MISUNDERSTANDING

According to legend, a Jewish family turned up at a funeral parlour in Glasgow to have one final look at their deceased father laid out. His daughter burst into tears when she noticed her dad had been dressed in a Rangers shirt, white shorts and blue socks. 'What have you done to my father?' she cried.

'I'm very sorry, Madam,' replied the undertaker. 'I was informed that his final request was to be buried in the Gazza strip.'

15

FLOWER OF SCOTLAND

⚽

*'At least the Scots have realistic expectations – they
expect to lose – and dedicate themselves to alcoholic
pleasures and exposing their genitals to foreigners
untutored in what Scots wear under their kilts.'*

Julian Birkinshaw and Simon Crainer,
Leadership the Sven-Göran Eriksson Way

It is fair to say that Scottish football has produced more than
its share of characters who have left an indelible imprint
on the sporting landscape, although not always in the way
they might have liked. This chapter celebrates the players,
managers, clubs and rivalries that make the country's football
culture unique.

THE DOC

One of Manchester United's most colourful managers was
Tommy Docherty. Among his other clubs was Villa. Of the
Aston Villa team of 1968, he said, 'Brains? Listen, there's
a lot of players who think manual labour is the Spanish
president.'

Tommy took the United job fresh from having guided
Scotland through the qualifying rounds for the 1974 World
Cup finals. It was a major achievement, as is evident from
the old joke: 'What do you call a Scotsman at the knockout
stages of a major football tournament? Referee.'

In typical Doc style, he boasted that managing United was the 'best job in football'. Moreover, he was prepared 'to walk from Scotland to Old Trafford for the job'. One wag was heard to mutter that that was probably because the Scottish FA was too mean to give him the train fare. The Doc's salary was £15,000 a year, twice as much as he had earned in the Scotland job.

He endeared himself to United fans with his comment on Manchester City's light-blue strip: 'There are three types of Oxo cubes: light brown for chicken stock, dark brown for beef stock and light blue for laughing stock.'

Few managers have proved more conclusively than Docherty that for wit, originality and generally great laughs, it really is a funny old game. Classic Doc-isms include:

'He said he was right behind me, so I told him I'd rather have him in front of me where I could see him.'

On Aston Villa chairman Doug Ellis

'The ideal board of directors should be made up of three men – two dead and one dying.'

'He can't run, he can't tackle and he can't head the ball. The only time he goes forward is for the toss.'

On Ray Wilkins

'He's not so much a coach as a hearse.'

On a fellow manager

'Robert Maxwell has just bought Brighton and Hove Albion, and he's furious to find it is only one club.'

'They serve a drink in Glasgow called the Souness – one half and you're off.'

'Preston? They're one of my old clubs. But then most of them are. I've had more clubs than Jack Nicklaus.'

'Some teams are so negative they should be sponsored by Kodak.'

'After the match, an official asked for two of my players to take a dope test. I offered him the referee.'

'Ron Atkinson couldn't make it. His hairdresser died . . . in 1946.'

'Football wasn't meant to be run by linesmen and air traffic control.'

Criticising the long-ball game

'He's got all the ability in the world, but there's something missing. He must be a brain donor. Brian [Little, Aston Villa manager] wanted a Colly, but all he got was a cabbage.'

On Stan Collymore

'We got such a run-around we were suffering from sunburned tongues.'

On a 7–0 defeat to Uruguay in the 1954 World Cup

'Mark Wright would get an injury if he went on *Question of Sport*.'

'There's a hell of a lot of politics in football. I don't think Henry Kissinger would have lasted 48 hours at Old Trafford.'

'They offered me a handshake of £10,000 to settle amicably. I told them they would have to be a lot more amicable than that.'

On leaving Preston North End

'The world's best tactician would make little difference with these players.'

Some encouraging words for the
Scotland national team in 2004

SEXY FOOTBALL

Sexy football is not, it has to be said, synonymous with Scotland in the same way as it is with, say, Brazil. However, in August 2003, Airdrie United chairman Jim Ballantyne made a bid to change that when he announced a sponsorship deal with Glasgow's Seventh Heaven lap-dancing club, having enjoyed its sights with some friends. The deal would bring billboards depicting scantily clad strippers to the Second Division side's New Broomfield ground. 'I rank it as one of my greatest achievements since I took over at Airdrie United,' said Ballantyne. 'I will be the only chairman in Scottish football who'll still be in seventh heaven even if we get gubbed 4–0 on a Saturday.'

EXOTIC CREATURES

One other strategy to bring more sexy football to Scotland has been the importation of a series of high-profile foreign players. By 2003, the SPL had become home to so many stars from abroad that journalist Tam Cowan joked, 'In midweek, both Old Firm line-ups had more foreign bodies than Willie Johnston's 1978 urine sample in Argentina.'

The colourful Italian player Paolo Di Canio was taken to Celtic fans' hearts when he played at Parkhead in the 1996–97 season. His most controversial moments came after he left Celtic, notably pushing referee Paul Alcock to the ground after being sent off while playing with Sheffield Wednesday in a match against Arsenal in 1998 and giving Fascist salutes while playing for Lazio in 2005.

However, his enduring legacy at Parkhead was a memorable chant, to the tune of 'That's Amore', in his honour:

> When the ball's in the net and it's not Jorge Cadete, it's Di Canio!
> When it sails through the air and it's not big Pierre, it's Di Canio!

When it goes like a bomb and it's not Andy Thom, it's
Di Canio!
When he goes all the way and it's not Paul McStay, it's
Di Canio!

HOOTS, MON

Scottish football has been the source of and the subject of
many a classic quote, including the following.

'Scotland are a good team with strong English character.'

Ruud Gullit

'The Old Firm match is the only one in the world where the
managers have to calm the interviewers down.'

The late, great Tommy Burns

'As recently as the late '70s, to woo our top players home,
the authorities introduced all-day drinking in Scottish pubs,
a valiant effort that succeeded only in enticing George Best
to Hibs.'

BBC Radio Scotland

'Some of the younger players think that lager makes you
invisible.'

Scotland manager Craig Brown

ROB MCLEAN: 'John Hartson is playing superbly today.'
SANDY CLARK: 'Yes, Rob, there is no one better today.'
MCLEAN: 'So, Sandy, who is your man of the match?'
CLARK: 'Alan Thompson.'

'Statistics are like miniskirts. They give you good ideas but
hide the important things.'

Former Aberdeen manager Ebbe Skovdahl

'Michael Owen has the legs of a salmon.'

Craig Brown

'Hearts 2, Motherwell 0. A good fight-back there by Motherwell, who were 2–0 down at one stage.'

Paddy Feeny, Saturday Special

'And there'll be more football in a moment, but first we've got the highlights of the Scottish League Cup final.'

Gary Newbon

'Hampden Park is the only ground in the world that looks the same in black and white as it does in colour.'

David Lacey, Guardian *sportswriter*

'Michael Owen is a parasite in the best possible sense of the word.'

Ally McCoist

'For years, I thought the club's name was Partick Thistle Nil.'

Billy Connolly

'He doesn't look like an international manager, but what does an international manager look like? A wee baldy man with bad knees, like me?'

Craig Brown on his Norwegian opposite number

'Anyone who takes drugs should be hammered.'

Andy Gray

'We don't get penalties at this club. If an opposition defender went at one of my players with a machete, cut his head off, dug a hole and buried him, then we might. Otherwise, no.'

Gordon Strachan at Coventry City

NO LOVE LOST

The rivalry between Rangers and Celtic fans has always been fierce. Here's just a sample of the jokes they make about their opposite numbers:

Q: What do Celtic fans use for contraception?
A: Their personalities.

Q: How many intelligent Rangers fans does it take to change a light bulb?
A: Both of them.

THE BRADY BUNCH

Arsenal legend Liam Brady had a spell managing Celtic in the early '90s. He was not the most popular Celtic boss of all time with the fans. However, Manchester City supporters appear to hold him in higher esteem as a manager, as their parody of Oasis's hit single 'Wonderwall' indicates: 'And maybe we should have gone for Liam Brady, 'cause after all, we got Alan Ball.'

John Barnes' brief reign as Celtic manager was doomed to a sad end when Celtic lost a cup tie 3–1 to First Division minnows Inverness Caledonian Thistle. It created a seismic shock in Scottish football. *The Sun* captured the moment brilliantly with its headline: 'Super Caley Go Ballistic, Celtic Are Atrocious'. Apparently, they'd been saving it up ever since Ally McCoist had starred for Rangers and only had to change a few letters.

TWO FOR ONE

Celtic fans are no slouches when it comes to making up chants. When Andy Goram was goalkeeper for Motherwell, media reports suggested that he was suffering from a mild form of schizophrenia. The next time Celtic came to Fir Park, the travelling fans sang in unison, 'There's only two Andy Gorams, two Andy Gorams!'

THE FAST AND THE FURIOUS

The traditional rivalry between Celtic and Rangers has added so much, good and bad, to Scottish football. Derby games between the two are no place for the faint-hearted.

A referee dies and finds himself stopped by St Peter at the pearly gates. He is told that only brave people who have performed heroic deeds and had the courage of their convictions could enter. If the ref could describe a situation in his life where he had shown all these characteristics, he would be allowed in. 'Well,' said the ref, 'I was in charge of a game between Celtic and Rangers. Rangers were a goal ahead, with seconds left in injury time. A Celtic forward made a break and weaved through the Rangers defence and scored a goal. He was offside, but as Celtic were clearly the better side, I ruled that he'd scored a legitimate goal.'

'My word, that was indeed brave of you, but I will have to check the facts in the celestial book,' says St Peter, and he goes off to look it up.

He returns with a puzzled look on his face and says, 'Sorry, but there's no record of this. Can you help me to trace it? When did it happen?'

The ref looks at his watch and replies, 'About ten minutes ago!'

PAYBACK

Craig Bellamy attracts a huge amount of comment. During his Celtic days, Rangers fans, perhaps embittered by his goal-scoring abilities or maybe because of his hotheadedness, liked to imply that he wasn't the sharpest tool in the box, and told the following joke.

One evening, Bellamy rings Martin O'Neill sounding rather upset and mumbles, 'I don't think I'll be at training this evening. I'm having trouble with this jigsaw puzzle and I'm not going anywhere until I've solved it. It's got a picture of a tiger on the box but none of the pieces seem to fit together.'

O'Neill, a bit annoyed, says, 'OK, give me five minutes and I'll come over and see what I can do.' When he reaches Bellamy's house, he goes into the kitchen where Craig is sitting at the table shuffling the orange pieces and looking confused.

O'Neill looks at the table, looks at Bellamy, and says, 'Craig, for God's sake, put the Frosties back in the box!'

A BRIDGE OVER TROUBLED WATERS

One day, Walter Smith is out jogging when he falls from a bridge into a very cold river. Three boys playing along the banks see the accident and without a second thought they jump in the water and drag the wet Rangers manager out of the river.

He says, 'Boys, you rescued the saviour of Scottish football today. You deserve a reward. You name it, I'll give it to you.'

The first boy says, 'Please, I'd like a ticket to Disneyland.'

'I'll personally hand it to you,' says Smith.

'I'd like an iPod,' the second boy says.

'I'll buy it myself and give it to you.'

'And I'd like an electric wheelchair,' says the third boy.

'I'll personally . . . wait a second, son, you're not disabled.'

'No, but I will be when my father finds out who I saved from drowning.'

CRASH LANDING

Celtic hero Paul McStay is on a plane with two Celtic supporters and a Rangers fan. The plane has too little fuel and too many people on it, and it begins to get into trouble. The pilot tells them that they need to lose two passengers. The first Celtic fan says, 'This is for you, Paul,' and jumps off.

The second Celtic fan says, 'This is for you, Paul,' and jumps off.

Then the Rangers fan says, 'This is for our lads,' and throws McStay off the plane.

DIRECT HIT

For many people, the voice of Scottish soccer is Roddy Forsyth because of his authoritative reports on radio. Roddy was in full flow at a Rangers match when he came to an abrupt halt. Explaining the cause of his problem, he said, 'Ach! Sorry, hang on a second. That's just ghastly! Sorry, a pigeon's just shit all over ma notes. Jesus! It's really big an' all. Ach, Jesus, it's on ma coat an' all!' Maybe the pigeon was a Celtic fan.

ASK AND YOU SHALL RECEIVE

A young Celtic fan was decorating his room, so he wrote to Parkhead and asked for 'stickers, brochures and penance'. A few days later, he received a package with a letter saying: 'We are sending you the brochure and stickers but would suggest that for penance you spend an hour a day with the Oxford Dictionary.'

A WAY WITH WORDS

At the end of the 2008–09 season when Gordon Strachan stepped down as Celtic manager, the probability is that it was the Scottish media rather than Celtic fans who were the saddest. In his managerial career, Strachan has had some interesting exchanges with the press.

REPORTER: 'So, Gordon, in what areas do you think Middlesbrough were better than you today?'
STRACHAN: 'What areas? Mainly that big green one out there.'

REPORTER: 'What about Agustín Delgado?'
STRACHAN: 'Listen, I've got more important things to think about than that. For instance, I've got a yoghurt to finish by today, the expiry date's today. That could be my priority rather than Delgado just now.'

REPORTER: 'Well, Gordon, all good things have to come to an end, and bang goes your unbeaten run this season. Can you take it?'
STRACHAN: 'No, I'm just going to crumble into a wreck. Go home, become an alcoholic and maybe throw myself off a bridge. Umm, I think I can take it, yeah.'

REPORTER: 'Things are looking positive, are they? There's no negative vibes or negative feelings?'
STRACHAN: 'Apart from yourself, we're all quite positive about here. I'm going to whack you over the head with a big stick. Down, negative man, down!'

REPORTER: 'Welcome to Southampton Football Club. Do you think you are the right man to turn things around?'
STRACHAN: 'No. I was asked if I thought I was the right man for the job and I said, "No, I think they should have got George Graham because I'm useless."'

REPORTER: 'Where will Marian Pahars fit into the team line-up?'
STRACHAN: 'Not telling you! It's a secret.'

REPORTER: 'What is your impression of Jermaine Pennant?'
STRACHAN: 'I don't do impressions.'

REPORTER: 'So, Gordon, any changes then?'
STRACHAN: 'Naw, still five foot six, ginger and a big nose.'

REPORTER: 'Gordon, can we have a quick word, please?'
STRACHAN: 'Velocity.'

GARY LINEKER: 'So, Gordon, if you were English, what formation would you play?'
STRACHAN: 'If I was English, I'd top myself!'

RUNAWAY TRAIN

On a train journey, an English international, a Scottish international, a spectacular-looking blonde and an older lady are sharing a compartment. The train passes through a dark tunnel and the unmistakable sound of a slap is heard. When they leave the tunnel, the Englishman has a big red slap mark on his cheek.

The blonde thinks, 'That horrible English footballer wanted to touch me, and by mistake he must have put his hand on the old lady, who must have slapped his face.'

The older lady thinks, 'This dirty English player laid his hands on the blonde and she smacked him.'

The English footballer thinks, 'That bloody Scot put his hand on the blonde and she hit me by accident.'

The Scottish player thinks, 'I hope there's another tunnel soon so I can smack that stupid English shit again.'

16

SHINY UNHAPPY PEOPLE

———⚽———

'The natural state of the football fan is bitter disappointment, no matter what the score.'

Nick Hornby, *Fever Pitch*

In the game's long history, fans have brought to football moments of mischief, mirth and mayhem. Following even the most successful team sometimes requires a fan to cultivate a pitch-black sense of humour if he's to see the funny side, and football's many local rivalries are a fertile breeding-ground for mickey-taking. This chapter pays homage to the dedication, passion and wit of that special breed, the football supporter.

TV TIMES

A Manchester City supporter has just been watching Man United on *Match of the Day*, and says to his wife, 'That was some programme. I'd only have changed one thing.'
  'What's that?'
  'The channel.'

MEDICAL MIRACLE

City fans were less than impressed with the way Cristiano Ronaldo would go to ground after physical contact and they suspected, perish the thought, that he might exaggerate the degree of pain he was suffering.

This gave rise to a story that after a particularly theatrical fall, Ronaldo thought he was dead. When the team doctor went onto the pitch, he found it tough to convince the player that he was still alive. Nothing seemed to work. Finally, the doctor tried one last approach. He took out his medical books and proceeded to show the United star that dead men don't bleed.

'Do you now agree that dead men don't bleed?' the doctor asked.

'Yes, I do,' Ronaldo replied.

'Very well, then,' the doctor said. He took out a pin and pricked Ronaldo's finger. Out came a trickle of blood. The doctor asked, 'What does that tell you?'

'Oh my goodness!' Ronaldo exclaimed as he stared incredulously at his finger. 'Dead men do bleed!'

Another story has Ronaldo going to the doctor and telling her that his body hurts wherever he touches it. 'Impossible,' says the doctor. 'Show me.'

He takes his finger, prods his elbow and screams in agony. He pushes his knee and screams, touches his ankle and screams.

'I thought so,' the doctor says. 'Your finger is broken.'

ONE FOR THE CITY FANS

Q: What do you call Sir Alex Ferguson up to his neck in sand?
A: Not enough sand.

PIG IGNORANT

A heavily built Newcastle fan, clad in his black-and-white striped shirt, is on his way to see his beloved team play away against Sunderland. For good luck, he brings a magpie. On the train, he winces when he sees a surly-looking Sunderland fan sitting down opposite him, wearing a T-shirt with the slogan 'I still love Roy Keane'.

The Sunderland fan leans forward and says, 'You'll never get into our wonderful stadium with that pig.'

The Newcastle fan contemptuously replies, 'Don't be stupid, man. This isn't a pig. This is our club mascot, a magpie.'

'Excuse me, I was talking to the magpie,' answers the Sunderland supporter.

PRIDE OF THE COUNTY

Randolph Churchill was giving an impassioned speech about the threat to the Lancashire cotton industry to a packed town hall. Intending to provide the answer 'the Conservative Party', Churchill asked the rhetorical question: 'And who is responsible for putting Lancashire where she is today?'

A voice came from the back of the hall: 'Blackburn Rovers!'

THE GENE POOL

Over a pint, two Mancunians from opposite sides of the great divide got into a debate. One asked the other to explain why he was such a dedicated City fan. He replied that his father and grandfather had both been true-blue Man City fans and he was carrying on the family tradition.

'That's it?' said his exasperated friend. 'What if your father and grandfather had been horse thieves?'

'Well . . . I suppose then I'd be a United fan like you.'

LAST WILL AND TESTAMENT

During an unsuccessful 2003–04 season, Liverpool fans were becoming thoroughly cheesed off with the manager. One supporter was making out his will, and his solicitor was surprised at one of the clauses he requested: 'To Gérard Houllier, I leave my clown suit. He will need it if he continues to manage as he has this season.'

The fans also joked that Houllier was going to a fancy-dress party as a pumpkin. He was hoping that at midnight he would turn into a coach.

UNFAIR GAME?

Spurs have been waiting for a league title for a long time. Arsenal fans claim that in the middle of the night the Tottenham chairman was woken up by a call from his local police station.

'I'm afraid the trophy room has been broken into, sir.'

Horrified, the chairman asks, 'Did they get the cups?'

'No, sir,' replies the policeman. 'They didn't go into the kitchen.'

AN IMPOSSIBLE SITUATION

Spurs fans are not renowned for their affection for Cesc Fàbregas, given his starring role for the old enemy, and have been known to pose the following brainteaser:

Q: You're a Spurs fan trapped in a room with a tiger, a rattlesnake and Cesc Fàbregas. You have a gun with two bullets. What should you do?

A: Shoot Fàbregas twice.

AN AGE-OLD ANIMOSITY

Since time immemorial, football fans have been complaining about referees. In fact, a recent archaeological dig near Old Trafford uncovered ancient scrolls inscribed with a series of conversations between a caveman and his wife. The priceless document recorded the prehistoric man moaning, 'I'm still annoyed about watching that match today. The referee was a wanker.'

His wife's response was: 'Will you ever get off your arse and do something productive like discover fire?'

OLD RIVALS

One of the best sources of comedy among football fans is the intensity of the feeling between rival fans. A case in point goes back to the 1970s and early '80s, when Liverpool's dominance ensured a bleak time for Everton fans. A sign near Goodison Park, erected by a local environmental group, read, 'You are now entering a nuclear-free zone'. A Liverpool fan had added a message of his own: 'You are now entering a trophy-free zone'.

In the mid-'80s, things changed when Howard Kendall led Everton to league and European titles. Some Liverpool fans couldn't handle the new footballing order, as this story illustrates. In 1985, a Liverpool family went into the city to do some Christmas shopping. In a sports shop, the son picked up an Everton shirt and said to his twin sister, 'I've decided to be an Everton supporter, and I'd like this jersey for Christmas.'

His sister, outraged by the suggestion, slapped him on the face and said, 'Go and talk to your mother.'

The boy walked off with the Everton shirt in hand and found his mother. 'Mummy dearest?'

'Yes, pet?'

'I've decided I'm going to be an Everton supporter, and I'd like this shirt for Christmas.'

The mother could barely speak with anger but eventually she gave him a smack and said, 'Go and talk to your father.'

Off he went with shirt in hand and found his father. 'Dad?'

'Yes, son?'

'I've decided to become an Everton supporter, and I'd like this shirt for Christmas.'

The father hit the son a thump on the head and said, 'No son of mine will ever wear that shirt.'

On the way home, the father asked the son if he had learned a lesson that day. The son thought for a moment before replying, 'Yes, I have. I've only been an Everton fan for an hour and already I hate you Liverpool f***ers!'

WINDOW OF OPPORTUNITY

As a Liverpool player, Robbie Fowler antagonised a lot of Everton fans with his strike rate for the Reds. In retaliation, they used to tell a story about the time Fowler went into a shop that sold curtains.

He tells the assistant that he would like to buy a pair of curtains in the Liverpool colours. The saleswoman shows him some patterns, and finally he makes his selection. The assistant asks what size the curtains are to be and Fowler replies, 'Fifteen inches.'

'Fifteen inches?' asks the assistant. 'That sounds very small. What room are they for?' Fowler tells her that they aren't for a room but for his computer. The surprised saleswoman replies, 'But, sir, computers don't need curtains!'

Fowler says, 'Hello? I've got Windows.'

HELLO, DARKNESS, MY OLD FRIEND

Magician Uri Geller is Exeter City co-chairman and former co-chairman of the Israeli national team. After Exeter were relegated from Divison Three to the Nationwide Conference in 2003, Geller, a veteran of the Six-Day War, showed the passion of the true fan when he made the slightly alarming statement: 'I haven't felt this bad since I killed a man.'

A LABOUR OF LOVE

Politicians have long been aware of how much football means to the voters and are more than happy to exploit national success for their own advantage. After England won the World Cup in 1966, the Prime Minister, Harold Wilson, quipped, 'Have you ever noticed how we only win the World Cup under a Labour government?'

PARTING IS SUCH SWEET SORROW

A Portsmouth fan had a ticket for the 2008 FA Cup final against Cardiff City but was seated right at the top of the stand, in the corner, with the worst possible view of the pitch. As the match started, he noticed one empty seat, beautifully positioned, exactly in front of the halfway line. Taking a chance, he raced down from the top of the stand.

'Excuse me, sir,' he said to the man sitting next to the empty seat, 'is anybody sitting there?'

'No,' replied the man. 'That seat's empty.'

'That's incredible! Who in their right mind would have a seat like this for the FA Cup final and not use it?'

'Well, actually the seat belongs to me,' replied the man. 'I was supposed to be here with my wife, but she passed away.'

'Oh, I'm sorry to hear that. That's terrible. But couldn't you find someone else – a friend or even a neighbour – to take the seat?'

The man shook his head. 'They've all gone to the funeral.'

A BIT OF AN ARSE

Three football fans are stuck on a desert island with only a cow to eat.

The first one says, 'I support Liverpool. I'll have the liver.'

The second says, 'I support Hartlepool. I'll have the heart.'

'I support Arsenal,' says the third. 'Thanks, but I'm not hungry.'

THAT FEELING OF ACHIEVEMENT

Long before he was fired, most England fans had lost faith in Steve McClaren. One of their stories had his secretary walking into the office to find the manager whooping and hollering.

'What is it, Mr McClaren?' she enquired.

'I've just finished a jigsaw puzzle in record time!' McClaren beamed.

'How long did it take you?'

'Well, the box said three to five years, but I did it in a month!'

FANDOM

'Whingers up and down the country' was one MP's uncharitable verdict on football fans. However, even if occasionally they clog up the airwaves of various radio stations bemoaning a referee's decision, for their wit alone they deserve to be indulged, as the following quotations prove.

'He makes even the most thrilling game sound like a coroner's inquest.'

Times *letter writer on Mark Lawrenson*

'The whole point about death, metaphorically speaking, is that it is almost bound to occur before the major trophies have been awarded.'

Nick Hornby, Fever Pitch

'Quinn, you're rubbish. In fact, you're so bad I could keep the ball off you for 90 minutes – in a telephone box.'

Arsenal fan to Niall Quinn during an incident
when his own fans refused to give him the ball back after
it went out for a throw-in at Highbury

'I think football would become an even better game if someone could invent a ball that kicks back.'

Eric Morecambe

'That's why we're going down!'

Southampton fans during a 3–1 reverse
to Nottingham Forest in 2009

'For those of you watching in black and white, Liverpool are the team with the ball.'

Liverpool supporters' joke

'Maggie isn't the only one with Crooks at No. 11.'

Spurs fans' banner, 1981

'I've had enough. As soon as I get home, I'm going to buy that club. I'm gonna walk in and say, "You f*** off. You f*** off. You, make me a cup of tea."'

Noel Gallagher getting frustrated with City's results in 1998

'Football causeth fighting, brawling, contention, quarrel-picking, murder, homicide, and a great effusion of blood, as daily experience teaches.'

Phillip Stubbes, seventeenth-century pamphleteer

'Blades' strip looks as if it was designed by Julian Clary when he had a migraine.'

Actor Sean Bean reacting to his beloved Sheffield United's strip

'One is not amused at that.'

The Queen's reported reaction when Sol Campbell's goal against Argentina was disallowed in 1998, ending England's World Cup dream

'We're gonna win 7–6!'

Hopeful Wolverhampton Wanderers fans, losing 6–0 with minutes to go in 2007

'White Hart Lane is a great place. The only thing wrong is the seats face the pitch.'

Les Dawson

'I would rather gouge my eyes out with a rusty spoon than have Dave O'Leary back as Leeds manager.'

Simon Jones of the Leeds United Independent Fans Association in 2003

'Can anything be done about entertaining us after the kick-off?'

> *A Stoke City fan gets down to the important stuff*
> *during a debate about pre-match entertainment*
> *at the club's annual meeting*

'Have ye no paid yer leccy bill?'

> *Aberdeen fans at Tynecastle when the*
> *floodlights went out in 2007*

FANS' ZONE

Kevin Baldwin's entertaining manual for fans *This Supporting Life: How to Be a Real Football Fan* (which suggests that the way to get into Old Trafford for free is to join a parachute team) includes an amusing spin on the crass commercialism to which clubs subject their fans with their frequent changes of strip for merchandising purposes. He suggests that the word 'UMBRO' on Man U's kit stands for 'United's Massively Big Rip-Off'. He also highlights the fact that sponsors whose names are initials have at times seemed tailor-made for the club, giving the following examples:

JVC (Arsenal): Just Very Cautious

LBC (Wimbledon): Long Ball Creed

NEC (Everton): Not Even Close

THE RED ARMY

If everyone, including United's players and manager, sometimes criticises Man U's fans (Roy Keane was the first to have a crack about prawn-sandwich eaters), then it's the United fans themselves who often dish out the harshest criticism of the team. In the 1990s, United's *Red Attitude* fanzine printed a photograph showing a plump, elderly nun kicking a football. The caption read 'David May Models New Team Strip'. Years later, one nostalgic wag was heard to say of May's time in the United defence, 'He was so fat he was on both sides of the family.'

THE NUMBERS GAME

Fanatical football fans often introduce their offspring to the game as early as possible. However, it can be a confusing game for the uninitiated. One young fan was watching *Match of the Day* with his dad and saw Liverpool score three goals against Derby in the first few minutes of the highlights package. He asked, 'How many is it up to?'

A FISHY TALE

In autumn 2002, when Stockport County were spiralling down Division Two, having been relegated from Division One the previous season, fans claimed that manager Carlton Palmer had invested in some tropical fish for the dressing-room to help relax the players. They would, said the supporters, link up perfectly with the rest of the squad. They were carp.

JOHNNY COME LATELY

Every cloud has a silver lining. One English fan saw some glimmer of consolation in England's habit of losing crunch matches in big tournaments after taking an early lead. He decided it was a sign that Englishmen were better lovers – because the English are the only ones who can stay on top for 45 minutes and still come second.

17

NICE THINGS LIVERPOOL FANS SAY ABOUT MANCHESTER UNITED

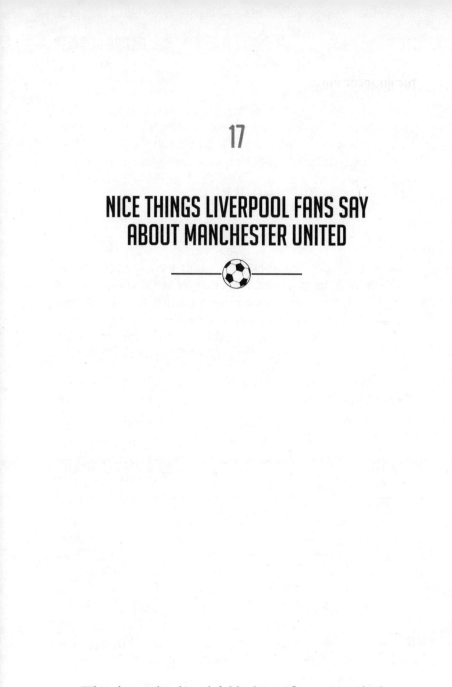

[This chapter has been left blank to reflect accurately the level of affection felt for Fergie's boys on Merseyside.]

18

HOLY WIT

Q: What's the difference between God and Roy Keane?
A: God doesn't think he's Roy Keane.

Jean-Paul Sartre wrote, 'When man understands himself as free and wishes to use his freedom, then his activity is play.' Sports and games have been an integral part of life for as long as there have been human beings. Through sport, people discover their strengths and find their limits. In games, they gain understanding of their relationships to other people and shape their communities.

Seen in this light, it is not that surprising that football and religion have overlapped in significant respects. To take just one example, the late Pope John Paul II enjoyed a successful stint as a goalkeeper before a higher calling took him away from the goalmouths of Poland. In 1991, another former goalkeeper, Coventry City's David Icke, went on Terry Wogan's television programme and calmly told the British public that he was the son of God.

The combination of football and religion has certainly generated some comic moments over the years, such as when Wigan striker Zaki kneeled in worship to say, 'I must thank God for this success. Credit also goes to Steve Bruce.'

HOD AND GOD

Of course, the most infamous link between football and religion was provided by Glenn Hoddle, whose view that disabilities were divine retribution for sins committed in people's past lives caused shock waves.

It all began innocently enough when Hoddle became a born-again Christian. This inspired a classic comment from the comedian Jasper Carrott: 'I hear Glenn Hoddle has found God. That must have been one hell of a pass!'

Back then, Hoddle restricted himself to such insightful comments about his chosen sport as: 'Football's about 90 minutes on the day; it's about tomorrows, really.'

During his time as England manager, things seemed to go off the rails when, among other things, Hoddle elevated his faith healer Eileen Drewery to daughter-of-God status: 'Jesus was a normal, run-of-the-mill sort of guy who had a genuine gift, just as Eileen has.' Hoddle asked the England players to pay her a visit. Rumour had it that when she put her hands on Ray Parlour and asked him what he most wanted, the Arsenal player replied, 'A short back and sides.'

The sports minister Tony Banks caught the mood of many people when he responded to Hoddle's notorious comments on reincarnation: 'If his theory is correct, he is in for real problems in the next life. He will probably be doomed to come back as Glenn Hoddle.'

Hoddle's attempt to dampen the outrage his remarks had caused showed that his grammar was as addled as his thinking: 'At this moment in time, I did not say them things.'

IN A PREVIOUS LIFE

Maybe Kevin Keegan believes in past lives, too. How else to explain his response when asked about one of his hobbies? 'I've had an interest in racing all my life – or longer, really.'

CROCODILE DUNDEE

In darkest Africa, there was a river infested with crocodiles. On the other side there was a tribe, and various groups of missionaries had travelled there in the hope of getting over to the other side to try to convert its members. However, they'd all either bottled out or been eaten by the crocodiles in the attempt. Then, in 2005, along came a group of missionary priests from Dundee who waded across the river without coming to any harm. On their return to Scotland, they revealed their secret. 'We wore T-shirts bearing the words "England – World Cup Champions 2006". Not even a crocodile was willing to swallow that!'

HOLY MOTHER

In 2000, John Hartson was on the point of signing for Spurs, but the transfer broke down because of a knee problem. His agent complained, bitterly and somewhat bafflingly, 'Their medical examination was so stringent only Mother Teresa would have passed it.'

WITH GOD ON OUR SIDE

The Irish writer Brian Moore began one of his short stories: 'In the beginning was the word, and the word was NO!' This sentence sums up the experience of a generation that concluded that Catholicism, Irish-style, was painfully negative and repressive. The Catholic ethos of the 1950s even affected the Irish soccer team. When communist Yugoslavia's national side came to Dalymount Park in October 1955, the Archbishop of Dublin was so incensed that he instructed all Roman Catholics to boycott the match. Despite his promptings, and demonstrations outside the ground, 22,000 fans attended. Apparently, God was on the side of the godless, as Yugoslavia won 4–1.

A NUN'S STORY

Packie Bonner was goalkeeper with Celtic in the 1980s and '90s. He had the prayers of the fans backing him. One woman took it to extremes. She lit a candle and put it over the place on the television set that Packie occupied. Then she changed it in the second half when Packie changed positions, to ensure that it would be burning over his head.

Packie's status as one of the top goalies in the world meant that he attracted huge adulation from people of all ages – including nuns. At one stage in his career, he had to go into hospital for a hernia operation. He was in the Bon Secours, a nuns' hospital and a very holy place. He had missed Mass on the Sunday, so he thought he would go during the week. It was all nuns but himself. He was being particularly pious that day. In most churches, people leave as soon as the priest is finished, but he was making sure he didn't make that mistake; he was going to stay as long as the nuns. As the priest said his final bit, a little nun came up beside Packie and said, 'Excuse me, Mr Bonner, I wonder if you would sign my Bible for me?' Packie's sure she's still doing penance somewhere for that!

THE SACRED SCRIPTURES

The juxtaposition of football and religion has resulted in some memorable lines.

'I'm not superstitious or anything like that, but I'll just hope that we'll play our best and put it in the lap of the gods.'

Arsenal manager Terry Neill

'Rovers want to nail down Duff.'

The Daily Mirror *announces that Damien Duff is being prepared to take the lead role in* The Imitation of Christ

'If I wanted to have an easy job . . . I would have stayed at Porto – beautiful blue chair, the UEFA Champions League trophy, God, and after God, me.'

José Mourinho

'The goal was scored a little bit by the hand of God, another bit by the head of Maradona.'

> *Maradona on his infamous goal against England in 1986.*
> *After he smashed a photographer's car window in 2000,*
> *he claimed, 'I did it with the hand of reason.'*

'When I saw the injury, I asked my God, "Look out for this player." I think God listened and he gave to Didier one more chance to play next month.'

> *Phil Scolari credits Drogba's recovery from a*
> *knee injury to divine intervention*

POSTER IN LIVERPOOL IN THE '60S: 'What would you do if Jesus returned among us?'
GRAFFITI: 'Move St John to inside-left!'

'Last time we got a penalty away from home, Christ was still a carpenter.'

> *Lenny Lawrence*

'Everything is written out for us – happiness and sadness – by Him. I believe there are two Christs. Him up there and me down here.'

> *Bulgarian international Hristo Stoichkov*

WHEN IN ROME

After the World Cup in 1990, Jack Charlton was the uncrowned king of Ireland, so when I got the opportunity to interview him for RTÉ radio, I thought all my Christmases had come at once. The first thing I noticed when I met Charlton was the speed with which he forgot my name. The conversation was peppered with phrases like 'the boy with the great left foot' and 'that nippy little winger' substituted for players' names. In Jack's distinctive Geordie brogue 'most' becomes 'moost' and 'goalkeeper' becomes 'gullkeepah'.

One of the consequences of Ireland's qualification for the quarter-finals of Italia '90 was a trip to Rome and an opportunity to meet the Pope – an experience Charlton will treasure for ever.

'I have to say it was a slightly tense occasion for me,' he told me. 'I am not a Catholic, so I found the ceremonial aspect a bit puzzling. We always had a priest in to say Mass for the Irish team and I attended them, but an event with the Pope is something completely different and a very big deal. I didn't know when to go forward and when to go back. I didn't want to embarrass myself or anybody else by making a cock-up. I knew it was a very proud moment for the players and all the staff. For some of them, it would be the icing on the cake of probably the biggest event of their football lives, but for others it would be the biggest event of their lives.

'The only thing was, the ceremony went on and on because there were so many delegations there and the Pope welcomed them in many different languages. It was also very hot, and I was petrified I would nod off and be shown in every newspaper in the world falling asleep when I was meeting the Pope!

'No matter what your religion is, the Vatican is a mighty organisation. The Pope is a very charismatic man. He is someone that you would like to meet regardless of your own beliefs. He said to me, "Ah, Mr Charlton. The boss." It was nice to bring a Catholic team to see the Pope. I have pictures at home showing me meeting him. I am very happy with those photos.'

I was afraid Big Jack would choke with laughter when I suggested that he could be canonised by the Irish people because of the success he achieved with the team. 'Canonisation? You couldn't do that to me – I'm a Protestant!'

I conducted my interview with Big Jack in a hotel room in Dublin when he was just out of the shower. All he was wearing was a bathrobe, which was a little too revealing for my comfort. Not wanting to delay the great man unnecessarily, when we had finished our chat, I hastily gathered together my recording gear. Too hastily, because when I got outside I discovered I had unwittingly taken one of his socks. It was a major moral dilemma: who else could say they had a souvenir of Jack Charlton's sock? Catholic guilt got the better of me, though, and I returned it, much to Jack's amusement. My one consolation is that I got closer than any other reporter to the sole of Jack Charlton.

JUST A MINUTE

After his meeting with the Pope, Big Jack was trying to understand the nature of the divine and asked God, 'God, how long is a million years to you?'

God was wearing his Ireland jersey and answered, 'A million years is like a minute.'

Then Jack asked, 'God, how much is a million pounds to you?'

And God replied, 'A million pounds is like a penny.'

Then Jack asked, 'God, could you give me a penny?'

And God said, 'In a minute.'

YOU'RE IN THE ARMY NOW

Big Jack is coming out of church one day, and as always the minister is standing at the door shaking hands as the congregation departs. He grabs Jack by the hand and pulls him aside, saying, 'You need to join the army of the Lord.'

Charlton replies, 'I'm already in the army of the Lord.'

The minister asks, 'In that case, how come I don't see you except for Christmas and Easter?'

Jack whispers, 'I'm in the secret service.'

BLESS ME, FATHER

A lorry driver who is a big Man United fan is heading out of Manchester on his way down to London when he sees a priest at the side of the road. Feeling it's his duty, he stops and offers him a lift. Further along, he sees Arsène Wenger at the side of the road and aims his lorry at him. At the last second, he thinks of the priest with him and realises he couldn't run over the Arsenal manager, so he swerves, but he hears a thump. Looking in the rear-view mirror, he can't see any sign of Arsène.

He begins to apologise to the priest for his behaviour. 'I'm sorry, Father. I barely missed that f*** . . . that man at the side of the road.'

The priest replies, 'Don't worry, my child. I got him with the door.'

THE GOOD BOOK

Gavin Peacock is English football's best-known born-again Christian. Having become a Christian as a teenager, during his time at QPR, he would organise prayer meetings for other footballers when he was at Chelsea in the mid-'90s. In 2008, he announced that he intended to study for an MA in Divinity at a seminary in Canada. A deeply religious Premiership footballer is a rare beast, meaning that Peacock had to put up with a few jokes.

One night, he returned home from appearing as a pundit on *Match of the Day* when he was startled by an intruder. He caught a man in the act of robbing his home and yelled, 'Stop! Acts 2:38!' ('Repent and be baptised in the name of Jesus Christ so that your sins may be forgiven.')

The burglar stopped in his tracks. Peacock calmly called the police and explained what he had done. As the officer cuffed the burglar to take him in, he asked, 'Why did you just stand there? All he did was shout scripture at you.'

'Scripture?' replied the burglar. 'He said he had an axe and two .38s!'

AN UNEXPECTED RESPONSE

Gavin Peacock is driving away from Stamford Bridge one day when he's stopped at a traffic light behind a car with a bumper sticker that says 'Honk if you love Jesus', so he toots his horn. The other driver leans out his window, makes a very impolite gesture and yells, 'Can't you see the light's still red, you moron?'

A MOTHER'S LOVE

In 1998, when David Beckham was sent off during England's World Cup match against Argentina for a petulant kick at an opponent, the *Daily Mirror*'s headline was 'Ten Heroic Lions, One Stupid Boy'. The fans were not impressed either, joking, 'When David Beckham was a boy, his mother prayed devoutly that he would grow up and play for England. So far, half of her prayer has been answered.'

19

THE FAME GAME

*'Very few of us have any idea of what life is
like living in a goldfish bowl, except, of course,
for those of us who are goldfish.'*

Graham Taylor

One of the occupational hazards of being a footballer is that everything about your life is fair game as far as the press are concerned. Some players rejoice in the spotlight; others find media intrusion a real pain. For the top players, it's an inescapable part of the equation: with talent and money comes fame – and all its attendant pitfalls.

THE FAMOUS FIVE

Footballers and managers have been known to believe their own publicity, as is confirmed by this top five big-headed pronouncements.

1. 'With me on the field, [Thierry] Henry and [Samuel] Eto'o would have to be on the bench.'

    Emmanuel Adebayor shows his modest side

2. 'I know I will get booed, but maybe in ten years' time I will be able to go back and the fans will think of me as a Birmingham great . . . they know that the club sold

one of their better players when they let me go. I did a fantastic job for them . . .'

Robbie Savage recalls his time
with Birmingham City

3. 'Please don't call me arrogant, but I'm a European champion and I think I am a special one.'

José Mourinho endears himself to
the British press in 2004

4. 'I'd compare myself to Zinedine Zidane in some ways. He's just a humble guy who happened to be the best and never wanted to be a star.'

Nicolas Anelka having difficulty
with the concept of 'humble'

5. 'People always say it's a shame someone as talented as Ryan Giggs, or George Best before him, never played in a World Cup or European Championship and I don't want my name to be added to that list.'

Barry Ferguson

THE STAMP OF DISAPPROVAL

The Royal Mail created a stamp featuring Cristiano Ronaldo to honour his achievements. However, the run of stamps seemed to be faulty. It emerged that they weren't sticking to envelopes. The enraged Postmaster General demanded a full investigation. After a month of testing, a special commission made the following findings:

*   the stamps were in perfect order;
*   there was nothing wrong with the applied adhesive;
*   people were spitting on the wrong side.

DIVINE STATUS

José Mourinho faces God at the Throne of Heaven with Sir Matt Busby and Bill Shankly. God says to them, 'Before granting you a place at my side, I must ask for your beliefs.'

Shanks stares God directly in the eye and says, 'I believe football is the meaning of life. Nothing else has brought so much joy to so many. I have devoted my life to spreading the gospel of football.'

God is moved by his passion and eloquence and says, 'You are a man of true faith. Sit by me at my right hand.'

He then turns to the former Manchester United manager. 'Now, my child, tell me what you believe in.'

Busby answers, 'I believe courage, bravery, loyalty, teamwork, dedication and commitment are the soul of life, and I dedicated my career to upholding those ideals.'

God replies, 'You have spoken well, my child. Sit by me at my left hand.'

Then he turns to José. 'And you, Mr Mourinho, what is it that you believe?'

José gives him the withering look that he usually reserves for referees who have the temerity to give a decision he disagrees with and replies, 'I believe that you are sitting in my chair.'

RUUD BOY

Another famous Continental import was Ruud Gullit. He didn't suffer from low self-esteem either. Asked about the cancellation of a planned meeting with Mandela in 1998, he replied, 'Nelson Mandela was as disappointed as I was.'

Gullit didn't have the easiest time when he was managing Newcastle. Even his maths let him down there: 'We must have had 99 per cent of the game. It was the other 3 per cent that cost us the match.'

PLAYING THE FAME GAME

The big reputations of the star players and managers have inspired some great quotes over the years.

'The FA have given me a pat on the back. I've taken violence off the terracing and onto the pitch.'

Vinnie Jones in 1995

'Vinnie Jones is as discreet as a scream in a cathedral.'

Frank McGhee

'Nobody cares if Le Saux is gay or not. It is the fact that he openly admits to reading *The Guardian* that makes him the most reviled man in football.'

Piers Morgan. Graeme Le Saux's reputation for being intellectual led to taunts about his supposed homosexuality.

'Throughout my career, I've been described as "cerebral". But I had to look up that word in the dictionary.'

Graeme Le Saux

'The last player to score a hat-trick in an FA Cup final was Stan Mortensen. He even had a final named after him – the Matthews final.'

Lawrie McMenemy

'I think I have something special that no one else has. I know Ronaldo is fast, he scores goals, has great technique, everything – but I am still a different player and in some ways I can be better than him.'

West Brom's Roman Bednar, getting competitive with £80-million player Cristiano Ronaldo

'It took a lot of bottle for Tony to own up.'

Ian Wright on the news that Tony Adams was an alcoholic

'Trapattoni is from a different galaxy to Venables. It's like comparing Abraham Lincoln to George W. Bush.'

Eamon Dunphy

'I'm sure people will always say I was the idiot who missed the penalty.'

Gareth Southgate after Euro '96

'Let's make him captain! Let's have him as president!'

Tony Adams taking the mickey out of the media's obsession with Michael Owen in 1998

'I've had worse things said about me than that. Tim Flowers once called me football's answer to Nigel Mansell. It doesn't affect me.'

Alan Shearer on his 'Mary Poppins' nickname

MOVIE STAR

Arsenal fans were not impressed by defender Philippe Senderos's part in the team's 4–2 defeat to Liverpool in the Champions League in 2008. They joked that he'd got an unexpected phone call promising a whole new level of fame. It was from Steven Spielberg. Having heard about Senderos's performance in the match, he wanted to cast him in his next film, *The Invisible Man*.

GUESS WHEN WE'RE COMING TO DINNER

As in any other walk of life, promotion can go to footballers' heads. The captain of one side newly promoted to the Championship liked to think that his celebrity status had rocketed. After an evening match, the team decided they wanted to go for a meal in the hottest new restaurant in town. However, everybody else wanted to eat there too, so they couldn't get a booking until ten thirty that night.

When the captain heard this, he was not happy and he convinced his mates that he could get an earlier booking using his position as captain. All the squad crowded around the telephone to learn from his negotiating skills.

'Hello, my friend booked a table with you earlier for ten thirty tonight, and I know it's a very busy Saturday night for you, but I was wondering if there was any possibility that you could fit us in earlier . . . Oh, no, I couldn't possibly allow you to go to a lot of trouble just for me . . . Well, the last thing I would want you to think is that I'm expecting any special treatment . . . Well, if you absolutely insist it's no trouble to you, that would be fantastic . . . Fine, fine. That's so good of you. I can't thank you enough. You've made all of us very happy. See you soon.'

His teammates were awestruck at his influence and they asked him what time they would now be eating. The captain announced with a flourish, 'Ten fifteen!'

20

BEAUTY AND THE BEAST

---⚽---

'With the greatest respect to women, football is the most
beautiful thing in the world.'

Croatia boss Slaven Bilic

Not surprisingly, the subject of beauty and related matters
raises its ugly head in the beautiful game. Not all the jokes and
quotes are pretty, though, so if you're particularly sensitive or
a passionate Newcastle fan, look away now.

BLIND DATE

With a few notable exceptions, footballers are not a particularly
good-looking breed, but for some reason poor Peter Beardsley
was often singled out as being particularly ill-favoured. The
Newcastle legend was nicknamed 'Quasimodo', and many a
joke was made at his expense.

One story had it that when Beardsley was a young man
his friend set him up on a blind date with a friend of his.
But Beardsley was a little worried about going out with
someone he had never seen before. 'What do I do if she's
really unattractive? I'll be stuck with her all night.'

'Don't worry,' his pal said. 'Just go and meet her first. If you
like what you see, then take her out. If you don't, just shout
"Aaaauuggghhh!" and fake an asthma attack.'

So that night Beardsley knocked at the girl's door and when she came out he was awestruck at how sexy she was. He was about to speak when the girl suddenly shouted: 'Aaaauuggghhh!'

IF LOOKS COULD KILL

Many of the jokes about Beardsley are cruel, but, as these lines show, they can also be pretty funny.

Peter Beardsley is so ugly that when he goes into a bank they turn off the security camera.

Kevin Keegan announced today that he would be bringing some new faces to St James' Park. Peter Beardsley is reported to have asked for one of them.

PETER BEARDSLEY: What's my best side?
PHOTOGRAPHER: You're sitting on it.

'He's the only player who when he appears on TV, Daleks hide behind the sofa.'

Nick Hancock

'As Peter Beardsley said to his wife on their wedding night, it's time to put on your blindfold and feel the sportsman.'

Stephen Fry, presenting a Sport Relief edition of They Think It's All Over

MAN IN THE MIRROR

Iain Dowie is another former player who's had the odd less than flattering photo taken in his time, giving rise to the following joke.

Quasimodo is sitting in his study feeling depressed about how ugly he is. Looking for some reassurance, he goes in search of Esmeralda. When he finds her, he asks her once again if he really is the ugliest man alive.

Esmeralda sighs and says, 'Look, why don't you go upstairs and ask the magic mirror who is the ugliest man alive? The mirror will answer your question once and for all.'

About five minutes later, a very pleased-looking Quasimodo bounces back down the stairs and gives Esmeralda a great big hug. 'Well, it's not me,' Quasimodo beamed. 'But who on earth is Iain Dowie?'

JUST DO IT

Of course, some players are confident enough in their looks to show the world their underwear – and not only David Beckham. After scoring a penalty to win the Women's World Cup in July 1999, American striker Brandi Chastain caused a sensation when she celebrated by ripping off her jersey, revealing her Nike sports bra. Shortly afterwards, New England midfielder Jim Rooney, having scored in a major league soccer game against San Jose, tore off his jersey, under which was a sports bra just like Brandi's. As if that wasn't enough, Landon Donovan equalised for the Earthquakes shortly afterwards and promptly whipped off his shirt to show the crowd that he too was sporting a bra in honour of Ms Chastain.

CHANGING TIMES

Tempora mutantur, nos et mutamur in illis. Times change and we change with them. One of the biggest changes in the world of football in recent years is the rise of the prima donna footballer who's as comfortable on a fashion shoot as on the pitch.

On the plane to Moscow before the Champions League final in 2008, Alex Ferguson was killing time by asking three of his players what they wanted their legacy to be.

'I'd like to be remembered as a great Manchester United player,' declares Ryan Giggs.

'I want my grandchildren to say, "He was a loyal family man,"' says Wayne Rooney modestly.

Turning to Cristiano Ronaldo, Sir Alex asks, 'So what would you like people to be saying about you in 50 years' time?'

'Me?' Ronaldo replied. 'I want them all to say, "He certainly looks good for his age."'

THE BEAUTIFUL GAME

Footballers' appearances, from their hairdos to their waistlines, have provoked a great deal of comment, some of it unkind, and some of it downright bizarre.

'Wolves keeper John Burridge has consciously modelled himself on the great Peter Shilton. Same sort of hairstyle.'

Byron Butler

'His face is in such a mess I'm going to bring him home and put him on the mantelpiece to keep the kids away from the fire.'

Dermot Keely, Shelbourne manager,
after an injury to one of his players

'I like defenders to be big, mean and ugly. Two out of three ain't bad. Are you mean as well?'

Ray Treacy, after his appointment as manager of
Shamrock Rovers, to defender Peter Eccles

'And so now the fair, long hair of Adrian Heath has been thrown into action.'

Bryon Butler has a hair-raising moment

'He had to come off. He had cramp in both legs and in his hair.'

Steve Bruce on Robbie Savage

'They had a couple of – what's a nice word for lumps? – big players up front. Lumps is too rude.'

Spurs' Martin Jol on Liverpool's strike force,
Peter Crouch and Fernando Morientes, in 2006

'Charles [Saatchi, her husband] dreamt I had an affair with Steve Coppell. I said to him, "Thanks a lot! You might have made it Mourinho!"'

Nigella Lawson

'Tell you what, if he was a lollipop, he'd be sucking himself.'

Rodney Marsh on José Mourinho

'I don't mind what you call me as long as you don't call me late for lunch.'

William 'Fatty' Foulke, England goalie, in 1901

THE SWEETEST SMILE

Brazilian ace Ronaldinho is known for his toothy grin and his talent for the beautiful game rather than for his natural beauty. When Liverpool fans saw him up close and personal during a match against Barcelona, they chanted to the tune of the conga:

> Cilla wants her teeth back,
> Cilla wants her teeth back,
> La la la la, la la la la.

Ronaldinho's teammate Ronaldo didn't have the best teeth either, leading Gary Lineker to comment: 'He must be the only man alive who can eat an apple through a tennis racket.'

BOSSY AND BEAUTIFUL?

With the exception of Birmingham City's Karren Brady, football bosses are not known for their beauty, as Eric Cantona perceptively noted: 'If I don't feel the environment is good, I don't want to be there. It's like with a woman. Sometimes you can't find love. Sometimes you can, but it's still not right; you want more, you want to give, you want to receive. I'm not sure that I would like to be with a woman who is like some of the chairmen I met.'

21

A GAME FOR ALL SEASONS

———⚽———

'If you took the goals out of it, I think it was pretty even.'

> West Ham manager Alan Curbishley reflects on a 4–0
> loss to Chelsea during the 2008–09 season

Every season tickles the funny bone in a unique way, and the 2008–09 season was no exception.

THE EUROZONE

Football fans got a welcome appetiser to the season in the form of Euro 2008. Of course, England didn't qualify for the finals, giving rise to a brainteaser:

Q: What do a three-pin plug and the England football team have in common?
A: They're both useless in Europe.

Nonetheless, it was arguably the most entertaining tournament since the 1970 World Cup. On the field, we saw the good, the bad and the beautiful. Off the field, we were entertained by some classic quotes.

'I would rather have my prostate gland expand to the size of a pumpkin than watch France win Euro 2008.'

> *Rod Liddle,* Sunday Times

'The defender was literally – literally – up his backside.'

> *Andy Townsend on the close attention paid*
> *to Jan Koller during a match against Turkey*

'I am not superstitious – it brings bad luck.'

> *France manager Raymond Domenech*

'He's absolutely indispensable. But so are all the others.'

> *Domenech on Karim Benzema*

'The Italians will be asking: would the Dutch have scored the second goal if they hadn't already got the first?'

> *Clive Tyldesley poses a mathematical conundrum*

'He's like six foot four of blancmange . . . more Swiss Toni than Luca Toni.'

> *Mark Lawrenson's take on Italy's misfiring striker*

'Czechoslovakia . . . the Republic of Czechoslovakia . . . the former Republic of Czechoslovakia.'

> *David Pleat struggles to name Portugal's opponents*

'Kroatastrophe!'

> *German newspaper* Bild's *headline*
> *after Germany lost to Croatia*

'I'm English, without a doubt. I will never say I'm not English. English born and bred. I'm Turkish, though.'

> *Colin Kazim-Richards goes through an identity crisis*

'Actually, none of the players are wearing earrings. Kjeldberg, with his contact lenses, is the closest we can get.'

> *John Motson*

'Croatia were a little bit tippy-tappy for me.'

Graeme Souness

MODERN-DAY SLAVERY

At the beginning of the 2008–09 season, there was much talk about Ronaldo's comments in the close season. He had been denied a move to Real Madrid, prompting Sepp Blatter to comment that players were enslaved by long contracts. When Ronaldo stated that he agreed with the FIFA president's view, the British press were up in arms that someone earning £120,000 a week should consider himself treated no better than a slave.

It was suggested that the time was ripe for a remake of the classic film *Spartacus*. The new version would be called *Ronaldocus* and relate the story of the famous slave revolt at Manicum Unitum. In the rousing final scene, when Governor Alexus Ferganus gathered the slaves together and demanded to know who was Ronaldocus, all the slaves would cry out with one voice, 'I am Ronaldocus,' before tumbling theatrically to the ground, clutching their ankles, howling in pain and demanding a penalty.

WAR OF WORDS

The Ronaldo saga sparked a lively debate between Old Trafford and Madrid. Real Madrid president Ramón Calderón said of Sir Alex, 'I'm not going to waste any time answering him. I admire his history, but recently he has gone a bit senile.'

Fergie's riposte? 'Would I get into a contract with that mob? Absolutely no chance. I wouldn't sell them a virus.' That sounded a lot like a no.

KEEN ON KEANE

After signing for Liverpool as Peter Crouch's replacement in July 2008, Robbie Keane was greeted by the Kop with:

He's quick, he's red, he talks like Father Ted,
Robbie Keane, Robbie Keane!

THE FLYING DUTCHMAN

In the opening week of the season, Steve McClaren found
that at last he was a hit. He became the number-one
attraction on YouTube after his Dutch side FC Twente lost
2–0 in the Champions League qualifiers to Arsenal. He gave
an interview in English with a pronounced Dutch accent.
English fans saw the irony. When he managed the national
team he normally seemed to be speaking double Dutch.

FOR FORK'S SAKE

When Spurs made their worst-ever start to the season, winning
2 out of a possible 24 points, having spent £77 million on new
players during the summer, the joke was: 'What's the difference
between Spurs and a fork? A fork has three points.'

It may have been their poor start that caused Spurs fans
to be so bitchy. Witness their abuse of West Ham's peroxide
blond striker Dean Ashton: 'You're just a fat Annie Lennox!'

IT'S OFFICIAL

It wasn't only opposition players the Spurs fans were laying
into, though. They also prepared a mock press release that
was none too flattering about their own side.

We regret that rumours attached to our players are true
– they are all crap. We have made our announcement in
the light of the overwhelming evidence in the Premiership
every week, which has made it impossible to defend our
players, although opposing teams have had no problems
defending against them.

GET TO THE POINT

In September 2008, Manchester City beat Portsmouth by a cricket score – well, an England cricket score. The 6–0 defeat inspired then Portsmouth manager Harry Redknapp to a bold new strategy: he sent his players on a team-building trip to Argos so that they could collect Premier points.

SHEIKH-ING ALL OVER

Manchester City fans were in seventh heaven when they became the richest club in England after their purchase by an oil billionaire. They responded in song:

> There's only one Sheikh Mansour,
> One Sheikh Mansour.
> Just fill up your car,
> And he'll buy us Kaka,
> Walking in a Mansour wonderland.

A DOG'S LIFE

Hull City shocked the football world by beating mighty Arsenal 2–1 at the Emirates Stadium, becoming only the second team to beat the Gunners at their new stadium in the league. Arsenal had taken the lead in the game thanks to an own goal from Paul McShane. Afterwards, Hull City fans asked each other a question:

Q: Why aren't the Arsenal team allowed to own a dog?
A: Because they can't hold on to a lead.

THE CUP RUNNETH OVER

Despite a good start to the Premier League season, Aston Villa were surprisingly dumped out of the Carling Cup at the first hurdle, losing at home to Queens Park Rangers. It prompted a revival of an old joke:

Q: What's the difference between the Villa team and a teabag?
A: The teabag stays in the cup longer.

GUESS WHICH

The 2008–09 season began spectacularly badly for Newcastle United, with the high-profile departure of 'the Messiah' Kevin Keegan, Terry Venables' refusal to become his successor, caretaker manager Joe Kinnear's infamous expletive-filled interview and the fans' anger with owner Mike Ashley.

Even before Keegan's departure, a general atmosphere of confusion was beginning to surround the club. When asked if he wanted to become Keegan's assistant, local hero Alan Shearer replied, 'One, I don't know if he wants a two, and two I'm not sure if I want to be one.' Chris Coleman's agent Alan Smith didn't improve matters when he was asked whether his client was likely to join Keegan at Newcastle: 'I have a feeling everyone is putting two and two together and making four.'

YOU SAY IT BEST WHEN YOU SAY NOTHING AT ALL

The 2008–09 season was a bumper one for comedy quotes. Here's the pick of the crop.

'They are conceding more goals than you would expect them to and they are letting them in at the other end.'

Ray Clemence on Spurs

'We scored three today, and ninety-nine times out of ten that means a win.'

Brighton assistant manager Dean White
after a draw with Cheltenham

'I have watched Gary Lineker never kick a ball in a game and still end up with two goals.'

Sir Alex Ferguson

'The most important space on a football field is the one between the players' ears.'

Watford manager Aidy Boothroyd

'There is a philosopher who says if you are too coherent, you run the risk of being an imbecile.'

Giovanni Trapattoni

'Our season is not beyond my wildest dreams – because they usually involve Elle Macpherson.'

Hull chairman Paul Duffen on their bright start to the season

'The team was happy with the news about Beckham, but what people don't know is that we'll also have George Clooney as coach and Brad Pitt as assistant manager.'

*Kakha Kaladze on the news that
Becks was to sign on loan for AC Milan*

'We've got to start winning games. That's the sixth game we've not managed to score, and that will always cause you problems.'

There're no flies on Bolton manager Gary Megson

'If you can't pass the ball properly, a bowl of pasta's not going to make that much difference.'

Harry Redknapp on the importance of a healthy diet

INTERVIEWER: 'Why did you take Wilshere off?'
ARSÈNE WENGER: 'It was past his bedtime.'

*Wenger explains his reasons for substituting 16-year-old Jack
Wilshere in a 3–0 Carling Cup victory over Wigan*

'They'll miss the physical presence of Van Hennegor, or whatever you call him . . . him from Castlemilk.'

*Alex Ferguson before a Champions League clash with Celtic, who
were having injury problems with Jan Vennegoor of Hesselink*

'People said I was pitting my wits against Sir Alex Ferguson, but it's like using a water pistol to take on a machine gun.'

Birmingham manager Alex McLeish
after a defeat at Old Trafford

'I am a dreamer and this has been one of my dreams.'

Manuel Pascali on the once-in-a-lifetime chance
of a dream move from Parma to . . . Kilmarnock

'Rafa Benitez is taking pity on Newcastle. He's bringing on Dirk Kuyt.'

Matt Le Tissier updates Sky Sports viewers on
Liverpool's demolition of Newcastle United

'The basics of what Barcelona did were very similar to our own, from the warm-ups to their set-piece work and passing drills. The only difference is the Barcelona lads could control the ball.'

Bradford City manager Stuart McCall
after watching a Barça training session

'I can't sleep at night for the crisis we are going through. How can I handle it when we won the Super Cup, are top of the Serie A table, in the Coppa Italia semi-final and the second round of the Champions League?'

A characteristically understated José Mourinho

'Gareth Jelleyman of Mansfield Town has been sent off. Hope he doesn't throw a wobbly!'

Jeff Stelling

'In the end, we lost a bad third goal because of an individual error by the goalkeeper. But I'm not going to point the finger of blame at anyone for that.'

Falkirk manager John Hughes adopts an
unusual approach to the blame game

'If I ever do a book, the title would have to be *Don't Google Me!*'

> *Craig Bellamy makes reference to his colourful past*

'Most of the players can't read anyway.'

> *Nigel Clough explains why he had a mural of inspirational quotes in the dressing-room painted over after he was appointed Derby County manager*

'Shay pulled out with a knee injury yesterday as did Insomnia . . . Insobia . . . eh, Charlie.'

> *Joe Kinnear, after Newcastle's defeat to Manchester City, struggles to pronounce Charles N'Zogbia's name. N'Zogbia was far from amused.*

'Why have Chelsea suffered so much since I left? Because I left.'

> *José Mourinho after the sacking of Big Phil Scolari*

'It won't faze him at all. One of his great attributes is that he doesn't think too much, so I think it will be OK.'

> *West Ham goalkeeper Robert Green on an international call-up for his teammate, Carlton Cole*

'For half a year, I was a bit morose. I just sat around, ate chocolate and watched porn. I didn't do much at all, really. I was all about chocolate and porn. But then I got a job gardening, and now I feel good. I know I can get a club in England.'

> *Australian Ljubo Milicevic and his unusual CV*

'If they wanted them smiling all the time, they should have employed Roy Chubby Brown.'

> *Roy Keane reflects on happy days with the Sunderland players*

'Scholes is now on his feet in front of us, but very gingerly.'

Clive Tyldesley

'It's an anagram, isn't it? If we get promoted, I'm a god. And if we don't, I'm a dog.'

Wolves manager Mick McCarthy

'I must admit I have a little trouble understanding Northerners. When we talk about football, the vocabulary is fairly limited, but when it moves away from that it becomes more difficult.'

Fabio Capello

SEEING THE FOREST FOR THE TREES

Newly rich Manchester City were humiliated in January 2009 when they lost 3–0 at home to Nottingham Forest, who were struggling badly in the Championship and had just sacked their manager Colin Calderwood after an abject loss to Doncaster.

The next day, City's manager Mark Hughes decides a novel strategy is needed to remotivate his team, so he summons all of the forwards, apart from Robinho, to a special screening in his office. He shows them an awe-inspiring DVD of Neil Armstrong walking on the moon, Sir Edmund Hillary at the top of Everest and Sir Ranulph Fiennes at the South Pole. Then he turns to the players and says: 'Each of you is paid tens of thousands a week. Can one of you tell me how we can watch people taking the first giant step on the moon, scaling Everest and exploring the Antarctic – and yet none of you useless f***ers can find your way into the Nottingham Forest penalty box?'

A few nights later, a Man City fan is driving home from a night in the pub. He's pulled over by a policeman. The officer says, 'I'm going to have to get you to blow into the bag.'

The driver pulls out a card from his pocket. It reads: 'Asthmatic. Don't take breath samples.'

The policeman says, 'I'm going to have to take a sample of your blood.'

He takes out a card from his pocket: 'Haemophiliac. Don't take blood samples.'

'Well, I'm going to have to take a urine sample, then.'

The motorist takes out another card from his pocket. This one reads: 'Member of Manchester City Supporters Club. Don't take the piss.'

THE BOY FROM BRAZIL

Manchester City faced a further crushing blow when their £100-million bid to sign Kaka failed. According to some estimates, the deal would have earned the AC Milan and Brazil superstar £2,976 an hour. The saga did yield some memorable quotes.

'I'd love to buy Kaka but they didn't take our £1-million bid seriously.'

Ricky Sbragia, Sunderland boss

'I think we would learn from him as much as he would learn from us.'

A debatable proposition from City
defender Nedum Onuoha

'We made an offer but it was turned down. We offered Stoke-on-Trent.'

Tony Pulis, Stoke manager

'If we haven't got Kaka, it's not the end of the world. We've got Craig Bellamy.'

City's executive chairman Garry Cook.
In all seriousness.

BARGAIN BASEMENT

Arsenal's season ended with a whimper when Manchester United's two quick goals in the second leg of the Champions League semi-final ended their hopes of bagging any silverware for another season. An advertisement appeared in the local paper three days later: 'For sale: Arsenal flag, good as new. Only used for seven minutes.'

Kind-hearted Spurs fans set up a helpline to assist Arsenal supporters with their trauma. The number was 0800 won nothing, won nothing, won nothing.

SO LONG

Despite the return of Geordie messiah Alan Shearer as Newcastle United manager, United were relegated on the last day of the season. A new riddle was born:

Q: What's the difference between Alan Shearer and Newcastle United?
A: Alan Shearer will still be on *Match of the Day* next season.

OUTWARD BOUND

The big story in June 2009 was Ronaldo's transfer to Real Madrid. The £80-million price tag was probably a fair reflection of his talents, at least in his own estimation: 'I am the first, second and third best player in the world,' he joked in 2008. 'But there are other good candidates like Kaka, Messi and Torres.'

He might have had his tongue in his cheek that time, but he certainly does seem to have a high opinion of himself. Asked to respond to criticism of his readiness to go to ground in 2007, the only explanation he could think of was: 'Maybe some people don't like me. Maybe I'm too good.' Former United player Eamon Dunphy is not Ronaldo's biggest fan. Before one big match between United and Roma, he stated, 'Ronaldo's a puffball who has never done it on the big occasion.' His judgement didn't look so sound, however, when United won 7–1, with Ronaldo scoring two goals. But is Ronaldo really worth £80 million? Dunphy's view on the transfer fee was: 'Eighty million quid? Sure, you could probably buy all of Ireland for that.'

THE LAST WORD

The 2009–10 season opened with a classic from Sam Allardyce. Asked about the possibility of selling Christopher Samba to Spurs, he replied, 'As far as I am concerned, there has been no contact with Tottenham – and I know that as I spoke to Harry Redknapp.' Meanwhile, Ian Holloway, newly appointed manager of Blackpool, was on promising form, commenting of a visit to former club Queens Park Rangers, 'If you met your ex-missus in a pub, would you have any feelings for her? Of course you would.'

THE FINAL WHISTLE

There are four types of people: happy people, sad people, very sad people and then people who collect funny sports quotations and stories. I belong to that endangered species.

As I sit here at the crossroads of the global interface (in other words, at my computer), my publisher rings.

He thinks my writing is all over.

It is now.

The GAA: An Oral History
John Scally

ISBN 9781845964436
£14.99 (paperback)

Available now

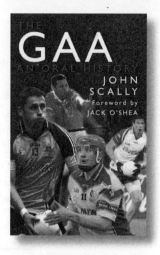

For more than 100 years, the GAA has been a fixed point in a fast-changing age. *The GAA: An Oral History* marks the 125th anniversary of the Association – as seen through the eyes of the key personalities who shaped it. They go behind the scenes and offer unique eyewitness accounts of the dramas on and off the pitch that captivated, enthralled and occasionally infuriated the nation.

More than 100 interviews with players and managers of the present and the past, such as Babs Keating, Jimmy Barry-Murphy, Ger Loughnane, D.J. Carey, Liam Griffin, Mick O'Dwyer, Colm O'Rourke, John O'Mahony, Joe Brolly and Matt Connor, are included. New light is shed on old controversies, fresh insights into the players and personalities that linger long in the memory are provided and the epic contests that turned the national games into the national soap opera are recounted by those who were there.

This celebration of the good, the bad and the beautiful of the GAA is a must for all sports fans.

Simple Goalkeeping Made Spectacular
Graham Joyce

ISBN 9781845964474
£8.99 (paperback)

Available now

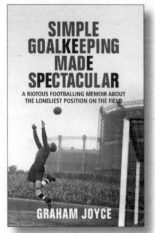

At the age of 52, a British writer gets the sudden call-up to play for England at the World Cup. The team can't find a goalkeeper and he's going to have to come out of retirement.

No, it's not a nightmare. The team is the England Writers XI, a chronically unskilled collection of scribblers who can't let go of their fantasies about being real footballers.

And so a raucous journey begins. En route to the finals in Italy, none other than Nigel Spackman, Gordon Banks, Lev Yashin and the scorpion-shaped shadow of René Higuita make their cameo appearances. From coats-down games in the park and schoolboy shield winners to fatherly advice and the violence of pub teams, this is the definitive guide to making it into a knackered old World Cup squad and putting the world to rights.

Funny, nostalgic and sometimes tragic, it's a book about why you take on the role of custodian of the goals. It's about the keeper's Technicolor shirt of dreams. It's about simple goalkeeping made spectacular.

Voices from the Back of the Bus
Stewart McKinney

ISBN 9781845965440
£16.99 (hardback)

Available October 2009

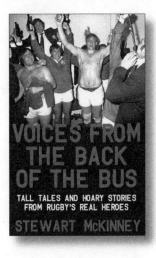

Voices from the Back of the Bus provides a rare behind-the-scenes look at international rugby at the height of a golden period.

With genuine warmth and much humour, more than 100 players – 54 of them British and Irish Lions – recall the scrapes, the games, the laughs, the glory and the gritty reality of the pre-professional game.

Author and former Lion Stewart McKinney has compiled priceless recollections of the glory days from an unprecedented number of legendary rugby names. The all-star cast includes: from England, Peter Wheeler, Jeff Probyn, Andy Ripley and Mick Skinner; from Ireland, Willie John McBride and Moss Keane; from Wales, Gareth Edwards, Phil Bennett and Mervyn Davies; and from Scotland, Andy Irvine and Ian McLauchlan, with contributions also made by New Zealand and South African rugby stars.

Packed with true rugby tales from the days when men played purely for the love of the game and of their nation, and multimillion-pound contracts and sponsorship deals were unheard of, *Voices from the Back of the Bus* is a refreshing, revealing and often hilarious collection that will inspire sports fans of all generations.

Around the World in GAA Days
Aaron Dunne

ISBN 9781845963637
£12.99 (paperback)

Available October 2009

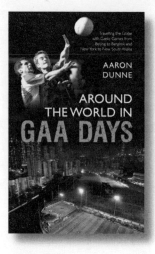

From its humble beginnings in the lobby of a Thurles hotel in the late nineteenth century, the GAA has grown to become the biggest amateur sporting organisation in the world, spreading its wings to all corners of the globe in the process.

Inspired by the mere mention of the Singapore Gaelic Lions GAA club during a Micheál Ó Muircheartaigh commentary at Croke Park, Aaron Dunne sets off to unveil as many as possible of the 200 or so tiny – and not so tiny – GAA clubs that are scattered about the world in the most unlikely of cities.

Aaron documents the rise and rise of Ireland's national games throughout the Gulf, Asia, Australasia and America, where hard-working expats are promoting the national sports and culture of Ireland. And, of course, keeping business booming in a few Irish bars-cum-clubhouses.

From the Dalian Wolfhounds' base in north-east China to the Irish experiment Down Under, here you will find all you ever wanted to know about the GAA abroad. So whether you're new to the international GAA scene, have been involved with clubs around the world or were blissfully unaware such a thing even existed – 'Failte' to a wild ride around the world in GAA days.